A WORLD WITHOUT A SAFETY NET:
Walking the Tightrope to Business Performance

A WORLD WITHOUT A SAFETY NET:
Walking the Tightrope to Business Performance

By

Frederick W. Croft

iUniverse, Inc.
New York   Bloomington

A World without A Safety Net
Walking the Tightrope to Business Performance

*The information, ideas, and suggestions in this book are not intended to
render professional advice. Before following any suggestions contained
in this book, you should consult your personal accountant or other
financial advisor. Neither the author nor the publisher shall be liable or
responsible for any loss or damage allegedly arising as a consequence of
your use or application of any information or suggestions in this book.*

iUniverse books may be ordered through booksellers or by contacting:

iUniverse
1663 Liberty Drive
Bloomington, IN 47403
www.iuniverse.com
1-800-Authors (1-800-288-4677)

*Because of the dynamic nature of the Internet, any Web addresses or links
contained in this book may have changed since publication and may no longer be
valid. The views expressed in this work are solely those of the author and do not
necessarily reflect the views of the publisher, and the publisher hereby disclaims
any responsibility for them.*

ISBN: 978-1-4401-5526-0 (pbk)
ISBN: 978-1-4401-5524-6 (hc)
ISBN: 978-1-4401-5525-3 (ebk)

Printed in the United States of America

iUniverse rev. date: 8/10/2009

TABLE OF CONTENTS

Seven: Execution: Do It Yourself 103

An examination of how to move from information to effective action, considering how to identify what's effective and the use of two commonly-used methods to achieve continuous improvement: Six Sigma and Lean (Toyota Manufacturing System)

Ten: Exit, Pursued by a Bear **209**
In which we consider how the change agent can stay alive through the restructuring process in a business that hates change and wants him deader than the proverbial doornail.

INTRODUCTION

WHY READ THIS BOOK?

This book was written because I needed it – and I needed it because my clients did. Successful restructuring efforts are driven by concepts and tools, and my restructuring clients weren't finding what they needed in existing publications. I couldn't find anything, either, so I cooked up my own. If I needed it and my clients needed it, the odds are – if you're a line manager in a mid-sized company – it includes things you'll need, too.

What's needed?

Two decades of restructuring work, both as senior management in public and private companies and as an operations consultant and advisor to private equity groups, have shown me there are several missing ingredients in the standard mix:

1. <u>More Real World Focus</u>: Universities are fine places. But the academic world is not the world faced by companies with performance and competitive problems. Concepts that sound fine on an Ivy League campus won't work with the battle-hardened managerial veterans of mid-sized companies' – or the banks, customers, employees and distribution channels those companies need to succeed. When I talk to these folks, I find them SICK TO %*&$!!!IN' DEATH of the facile

phrases, politically correct baloney, fashionable catchphrases and style manual footnotes they get from MBA textbooks and business cable soundbites.No more PowerPoint shows; no more guys with sincere suits and platitudes. They need tools they can apply, developed by people who understand their problems.They need things they can use NOW. They need ammo, not term paper baloney.Specifically, they need (a.) concepts that give them new solutions and options, and (b.) operating tools that will help them execute.

2.   <u>More Real World Tools</u>: This is a tricky subject. Many of the tools that we've used to manage businesses over the last two decades – notably Generally Accepted Accounting Principles ("GAAP"), the public accounting/rating agency certification system that led to scandals ranging from the Bear Stearns debacle through to the massive failure of Moody's and S & P to identify the dangers in subprime derivatives, and the tendency to focus on financial engineering rather than building corporate value – have stopped working.The old tools failed; the falcons cannot hear the falconers; and we're headed at Warp Factor Seven to a brave new financial world that most businesses don't have the systems to understand. In the chapters ahead, we'll examine specific tools and strategies that my clients and I have used to cut through the fog of business war to see where we're making or losing money, and how to improve quality as business performance.

3.   <u>Real World Global Management</u>: Offshoring isn't going away.Most businesses have accepted that

and have moved basic fabrication across the water, but few have the capability to manage what happens in those foreign factories

4. <u>More Real Value</u>: We've reached the end of the Era of Financial Engineering. Successful managers in the years ahead will move from using accounting tricks to create illusory value to building real worth: assets, brands, intellectual property, higher gross margins, durable sales channels and all the rest of it. The following chapters contain processes and tools that will help you build real worth.

WHO SHOULD READ IT?

If you're a line manager or executive and you think the world is going just swell and business is great, save your money. If an MBA gave you everything you need to succeed, you've got it covered.

But what if you don't?

If you need tools to make better decisions – and to understand when those decisions are or aren't working – you should read this. If you need to understand where you're actually making or losing money (not just what shows up at gross levels in a GAAP statement), you need to read this. If you need to execute, to run your business effectively, improve product/service quality, and build higher gross margin, you should read this.

WHO AM I?

I'll give you the standard text from my consulting firm handouts:

"Frederick W. Croft is Managing Partner of PVM Partners LLC, a Los Angeles-based project management and operations firm working with public and private corporations in the US, Asia and Europe, private equity firms and investors to create and maximize corporate value. He served as CEO, COO and CFO in various public and private companies in the manufacturing, distribution, service and health care industries, previously managed engagements in the Management Consulting Group in KPMG Peat Marwick, and ran a Lloyds of London syndicate. He's lectured for the California Society of Certified Public Accountants, the University of California at Los Angeles, and the University of Southern California. He is a co-author of the UCLA Anderson Forecast's "Solutions For Our State", and received a White House Letter of Commendation from the Clinton Administration for his economic analyses."

What does that mean to you? I have some qualifications. I've been successfully creating better business performance for several decades. I'm a doer, not a talker. I've run troubled companies and gotten them out of trouble. The concepts and tools included here have been tested in a number of problem businesses are worked. The tools that worked for me can work for you, if you're a line manager in a mid-sized company and find that you need help in creating value.

LANGUAGE AND REALITY

A word of warning. This is a working text, and I've written it in the language of a production environment. If you want a batch of footnotes and academic citations, you should find yourself another book. My clients consistently agree that, for a line manager, a bunch of academic nonsense obscures the concepts and tools, makes the text harder to read and refer to in crisis situations, and generally decreases the value of the text to the line managerial user. They don't want it.

For the literary theoreticians in the audience, I'm avoiding standard academic format for a good reason: it's a system designed to reinforce "trust" and "expert wisdom", which I believe are primary reasons that we've suffered loss of business value and seen so many investments managed by "the best and the brightest" flushed down the sanitary facility in the last few years. I don't want you to trust. Don't trust experts; don't trust certifications – and don't trust me, either.

Hunter Thompson (a man seldom cited in business texts) noted that the idea behind "Gonzo Journalism" was that it was valuable to use language to destroy the dangerous illusion that the journalist was giving you the "absolute truth". This would (hopefully) force you to actually THINK FOR YOURSELF. I think this is equally applicable in business – and the utter failure of experts and standard techniques in the Great Subprime Meltdown indicates that skepticism should be encouraged by any means necessary.

So this doesn't look academic. It's not always polite. But it IS real, and the concepts and tools included in it have proved repeatedly useful.

You want polite, you should go read Miss Manners.

Are You Sufficiently Shocked And Appalled?

God, I hope so. Because, if you are, you're going to not blindly trust everything I'm telling you, will start thinking for yourself – and I'll have succeeded.

Enough said. Let's cut to the chase.

I
AFTER THE FALL

A funny thing happened after the Great Subprime Meltdown. Everything changed.And I'm not the only person who thinks this, either. "Staying rich in this future world will require strategies that reflect this altered vision of [lower] global economic growth and delevered financial markets", notes PIMCO's Bill Gross in his May 2009 newsletter."The world, in my opinion, is changing and is shifting away from the financial types to producers of real goods, and this is going to last for several decades" agrees former Quantum Fund principal Jim Rogers on his blog, before suggesting that ex-investment bankers may want to consider new careers as farmers and taxi drivers. Hong Kong-based fund manager Marc Faber suspects that the only areas where the United States has competitive advantage are "beer and prostitutes".

All right, then!

If you're a line manager in a mid-sized business, you're working through a funny time in financial history. The rule book's in the trash; the experts are in the penalty box, and it's quite likely that you're wondering "What the $*&%!!! do I do next?" There are few certainties left to us, but I'll give you a few observations that may prove useful.

SOME THINGS TO THINK ABOUT

1. <u>The Era of Cheap Money is Over</u>: The U.S. has, for good or ill, piled on a mountain of new debt to bail out assorted investment firms that couldn't invest, auto companies that couldn't sell cars, insurers who couldn't manage risk, state programs that didn't want to shut down and various other good and worthy recipients. It's done this at the same time that my occasional clients the Peoples' Republic of China are expressing concern over the impact of inflation on the dollar and cutting deals that will allow them to use their own currency in deals with Brazil, Russia and Japan rather than rely on the old and outmoded international reserve currency, the dollar. It's probable that this will lower the demand for new U.S. debt issues, which increases the probability that the U.S. will run the presses and the ugly specter of inflation will stalk the land.

    What does this mean for the mid-sized company executive? It means you'll pay more for the money you borrow. It means that tactic that worked with 5% interest won't work with 10%.It means that you'll need to generate more of your working cash flow from internal operations, or you'll face return on investment problems, disgruntled shareholders, and general bad times.

2. <u>Global Competition isn't Going Away</u>: Global trade isn't about industry.

It's about gadgets and home furnishings and Harry Potter and Parisian dance tracks and Dyson vacuum cleaners. It's about medical transcription done in India, and software coding in Islamabad. It's "Slumdog Millionaire" instead of Hollywood. Some "Big Four" accounting firms have their clients' financial statements assembled in Manila.Major insurance carriers settle claims in Dublin. Paralegal work is routinely e-mailed back and forth with Bangalore, and the world's largest and highest-quality cardiac center is now in Karnataka.

International trade used to be limited by the factors of transportation cost and shipping time. Air freight and low cost container shipments have changed all of that for physical objects. But most of us don't work with physical objects; we work in service and intangibles industries.For these categories, the Internet brings the whole world into the same room at the speed of light (or somewhat less, if your ISP is like mine ...) The great barriers of time and transport vanish into air, and being the friendly local tradesman doesn't mean so much to your cost-conscious customers.

Products aren't necessarily the product of one company or one country these days: it's quite simple for a local marketer with a good idea and some connections to link up with foreign manufacturers, development resources – whatever they need.
So don't think of your competition as the Chinese: think of it as your uncle Louie the Sales Guy down the street, PLUS IBM and all of its resources, plus some guy with a math PhD in a garage in Vientiane

whose monthly income is slightly less than a single topping Dominos pizza, all attempting to undercut you with higher-quality products, better sales pitches and lower costs of capital.

Facing this aggressive, adaptive competition, it's increasingly necessary for producers to move fast enough to access consumer desires before they've moved on to something else. In the ever-applicable words of Diamond David Lee Roth, product lifecycles (like rock stardom) can be described as "here today, gone later today." Useful working life (over which you recoup your invested capital and maybe even a bit of profit) is often measured in weeks.

What's a mid-sized company executive supposed to do about this? They're management, so they're supposed to manage. They need to build efficiency and quality (which are two sides of the same coin) to a point where they're world-class competitive.

3.   Labor Cost Makes a Profound Difference:
We in the U.S. choose to have minimum wages. We choose to have fringe benefits and unemployment coverage and OSHA.

We did a project for a private equity firm about a year ago. The equity firm owned an auto aftermarket company that manufactured goods in three plants: one in the U.S., one in Tijuana, and one in Guangzhou, PRC. We analyzed loaded labor costs for the three plants as part of our work, and the differences in labor costs show the magnitude of the labor issue for manufacturers:

U.S.	$25.50 per hour
Tijuana	$ 5.50 per hour
Guangzhou	$ 1.50 per hour

The reminbi (the PRC currency) has gone up a bit since then, but the effective labor cost per hour still is below $1.70 per hour. A firm using U.S. labor has a fifteen-to-one labor cost hurdle to overcome if it's facing competitors who manufacture in the PRC. US workers may be better than the ones in Guangzhou – but are they fifteen times better? (For what it's worth, the Guangzhou plant in our study had lower scrap and rework rates than the other facilities ...)

U.S. customers may not pay more for a "Made in USA" label. If they're forced to pay equivalent prices by a tariff or import barrier, aren't the majority of Americans (i.e., the consumers who don't work in auto manufacturing facilities) suffering by being forced to subsidize uncompetitive workers through overpriced goods? And might they not express their annoyance politically? There are a lot more Wal-Mart shoppers than there are U.S. factory workers ...

Customers aren't the only folks weighing their options. There are several billion people who don't live in the United States, but would like to make progress toward U.S. living standards.
One way that they can do this is taking jobs that U.S. citizens aren't willing to do. For most of the

world, OSHA and unemployment coverages are luxuries that they'll do without – they're happy to get more than the dollar a day that the locals will pay them.

Ah, you say that the PRC has plant closures and job losses now that we've had the Great Worldwide Meltdown and the world economy's feeling our pain.True enough. Do you think that will make the Chinese LESS hungry? Will all the Indians and Vietnamese who've seen their glimpse of the Gold Mountain say "The U.S. consumer's got less money, so we'll just forget it and head back to the rice paddy"?   Or will they say "We can go lower on labor cost than our competitors, and we'll fight for whatever market survives"?

And labor costs aren't simply a function of labor. They're a trade-off. Example: auto parks. A few years ago, these were the domain of energetic young fellows who rushed about acting as valets, taking your car and getting it for you when you were ready to leave, and collecting whatever fees the parking facility charged you. That's not happening any more – now you press the button for a parking ticket, and feed it into the electronic payment module when you're ready to leave so the barrier will go up and you can leave the structure. Not a valet in sight; you end up talking by phone if the payment module screws up.

This wasn't the result of a neutron bomb targeting valets.Asian valets aren't undercutting the local boys, either.It's the natural end point for a system where people will pay limited amounts for their

6

ability to park a car – or for anything else that they want. They'll go for automation if they can't get cheap labor.

Back to the viewpoint of our mid-sized company manager. What he takes away from this is that good intentions lose when they fight it out with markets. Efficiency is a requirement, not a choice. If you're not efficient, the Wal-Mart customers of the world – i.e., the vast majority – will buy from someone who is.

4.   The greener the U.S., the bigger problem for many U.S. industries: This one's a conundrum for me, personally – I'm a significant shareholder in an environmentally-driven enterprise, and I believe we have to address the real national security, quality of life and sustainability concerns which drive the movement toward eco-sensitive products. Green industry has been promoted as the savior of the American economy. Maybe.

We in the United States don't want to live next door to toxic metal tailings, carcinogenic dye dumps or many of the more colorful aspects of Third World manufacturing hot spots. Since I don't make a living off of that stuff, I'm all in favor of a hard-core Green position that preserves my nice little suburban neighborhood.

But we've exported the U.S. consumer electronics manufacturing industry, in part, because it involves a lot of weird metal tailings and acids (circuit board manufacture), lead (CRT screens) and other fun stuff. No more Zenith televisions or RCA radios.

7

Industrial paint shops for anything from furniture to custom cars are becoming difficult to create or maintain in this country because of environmental and OSHA requirements. The same thing's true for batteries and power train products.

And then there's research and development.
It's no accident that the industrial parks around Shanghai are studded with bio-research and drug development facilities. The PRC does have drug and consumer neutraceutical products legislation, but it's not anywhere near as overwhelming as the FDA in this country.

We've made a choice. Since I'm not too interested in growing another head from exposure to the output of the bio-dump down the street, I'm on board with this cultural decision. But, with this same decision, we've also elected to export drug and new products development to parts of the world where they aren't quite as fastidious. We need to develop other goods and services to sell them that will pick up the slack.

Where does this put our mid-sized company line executive? It probably puts him in the "deeply confused" column. On one hand, the Boone Pickens argument ("We're sending a trillion dollars a year to people who don't like us") has national security implications: can the U.S. afford to have its energy needs driven by the same folks who fund Al Quaeda? On the other hand, betting that the U.S. economy can be driven by a Green Renaissance – when we're competing with areas such as the U.K. and the PRC who have, in many areas, more experience and a deeper skill base than we do – seems risky. Again, we come back to the need for companies to be world-class competitive, to be able to slug it out and win business, whether it's in the U.S. or elsewhere.

5. <u>The Rate of Change</u>: The global economy is more fragile, less stable, and more subject to change than it's ever been. When Best Buy's got permanent sourcing people in Shanghai and my local print shop uses Alibaba, local competition is world competition.

    There's also the "interconnected network" problem, which suggests that China's problems are ours – and vice versa – in a multinational economy. The actual interconnected network problem (which was recently researched by someone named Felix Reed-Tsochas at Oxford) found that, while network clusters are very resilient when the network is expanding, the network becomes very dependent on its primary relationships when it contracts, making the shrinking network far more fragile. The implications, in a world where the PRC has now started its own half-trillion dollar internal bailout even when it's sitting on the world's largest foreign currency slush fund, emphasize that there's no one big enough or well-funded enough to step away from the global economy. The shot heard round the world was the one through the head of every one of the world's economies the minute one of them has a problem.

OMIGOD!

Is U.S. business completely screwed? Nope.We have the ability to compete and win in corporate competition.

In spite of Bollywood and all those effete French auteurs, Hollywood rules the motion picture universe. California rules the product design universe, with IDEO and Astro and BMW Designworks. On the fashion front, established US lines including Ralph Lauren and DKNY and young brands such as Sean John, Ed Hardy, Juicy and American Apparel compete quite effectively with foreign labels.Just look at the shops in Shanghai and see how much Asian fashion is driven by U.S. firms: you'll see more Nike logos and Kobe jerseys than you'll find in Los Angeles. Recorded music is dead as the pyramids, but U.S. acts from Madonna to Justin Timberlake to Black Eyed Peas still pull top numbers in the live performance world.

The Internet is dominated by Google, by Facebook, by eBay, by MySpace, YouTube – all U.S. companies. Microsoft and Oracle dominate software. American firms are still major forces in aerospace, even after decades of European subsidies for Airbus. Emerging technologies from nanotech to open source software ventures are U.S. dominated. Seven out of the ten largest private equity operations in the world are U.S. companies. Mattel remains a top toy manufacturer. WalMart and McDonalds are showing foreign retailers how it's done by taking profits from Asian and European customers and sending them back here to America.

Global competition is working out just fine for many U.S. companies. How do they do it? What are they doing that you're not?

Those are questions we're going to examine. Some of that examination will come through practices and experiences of successful U.S./global multinational companies. Some of it will come from specific situations I've encountered in several decades of helping clients who faced global competition and global markets issues adapt to them and resolve problems. All of it will provide line managers in mid-sized companies with some options for managing more effectively in a competitive world.

II
REALITY AND HALLUCINATION
IN MODERN BUSINESS

Business as usual, as we've seen from the issues in the last chapter, is business headed for liquidation. If your business is going to live long and prosper, you want business that's NOT usual. You want business that's expanding and increasing gross margin and making your customers faint with desire.

This will require us to, as the old Apple ads urged us, think different. Thinking different is a skill that grows with practice.

One moment. Since we're going to be looking at various strategies, let's start thinking different by administering a vision test for spotting them. An intellectual vision test; one which evaluates your response to unexpected variations on standard themes. A test that goes like this:

A SIMPLE TEST

At last! After all those years of sixty hour workweeks, pissed-off spouses and clawing your way up the corporate ladder, you get your shot at your own personal Horatio

Alger story. The top job: CEO for a little regional logistics company, an air freighting operation in an emerging Asian market. This could be IT, the moment you've worked for over your entire career.

So you take it. You've got the top slot.

But then you wake up and find yourself in this Third World hellhole, a small steamy, malarial island somewhere off New Guinea. Hundred degrees and ninety-five percent humidity at midnight kind of steamy; hot and cold running tsetse flies; the wet smell of monsoon mornings and rotting ginkgo palms … Your staff are all Watap tribesmen, teeth filed, cheeks scarred and eyelids tattooed as a reminder of their off-hours hobbies: extreme piercings and tryouts for the Olympic headhunting team. You find your balance sheet assets consist of a torch-lined, unpaved airstrip and a collection of wicker "planes" and bamboo "control towers." Everyone tells you (in their colorful, barely-comprehensible tribal patois) that the shipments – the valuable cargos of plasma TVs and Jeeps and air conditioners and (of course) automatic rifles – will be arriving any time now air freight special delivery courtesy of a mysterious Savior named "John Frum." And as they wait, the tribesmen build wicker offices and desks where they sit for days at a time shuffling banana leaves back and forth while waiting for the arrival of Big John and the Sacred Elder Gods.

Hey, wait a minute! You're not running a business – you're running a Cargo Cult!

Here comes the test – how do you feel about that?

It's very easy to assume that standard answers apply when something looks like a standard situation. It's also very easy to get yourself into a hellacious mess when you do so. Would you rather live with said hellaciousness than rock the boat?

Our test scenario is no longer limited to Palau Karang island, and plenty of American MBAs go through paper shuffling exercises just as pointless as those rustling banana leaves and crumbling bamboo control towers. These days, too many executives find themselves running Cargo Cults and believing that some form of MBA "magic" or "financial engineering" or "smartest guys in the room" will save them from having to deliver corporate performance in an unforgiving business environment. That won't create value for their shareholders, and it won't keep their business alive.

Unlike the Loving' Spoonful in the Boomer-Rock classic, I don't believe in magic, and neither do the financial markets. They believe in smart decisions. They believe in information, not data. They believe in adaptability. They believe in managing operating risk. There are many of us who believe that we'll all have to be much more effective executives or we'll be much more unemployed executives.

The alternative? Cargo Cult time, which works out better for Neolithic tribesmen than for contemporary executives. Cargo religion isn't limited to the guys with bones through their noses; there are huge chunks of American business being killed by primitive rituals and unthinking worship of industry standard approaches.

WHAT IS TO BE DONE?

Let's start with a few conceptual tools, each of which indicates problems we'll have to resolve:

- Accounting is set up for loan underwriting, not corporate operation.

- Expert certification, the process underlying

financial processes from bond underwriting to loan management, turned out to be inherently corrupt – and corrupt structurally, so merely punishing the evil-doers won't fix it.

- Production operations are set up using mass production, not effective production.

- Management talks strategy, but measures tactically.

- Management talks customer-driven, but acts customer-oblivious.

As the poet Baudelaire once observed in his fashionably cynical Gallic manner, "To live outside the law, you must be honest." To live in the lawless world of trans-national markets and hungry competitors, you must also be honest. And honesty starts with honest data, honest accounting, and honest analyses of your situation. It culminates in being honest with yourself.

We can start with some honesty about the shortcomings in our financial management tools. There has been a revolution in accounting procedures in the past fifteen years – and it hasn't been a positive revolution for anyone except CEOs willing to pay their accounting firms to come up with esoteric methods of concealing wretched performance – and for the accounting firms willing and eager to take their money.It's time for a counter-revolution.

Once we're through with accounting and finance, we can look at the inertia and confusion of most production environments. We then move on to the general weakness in logistics management and the general speciousness of much "strategic planning."

Most mid-sized businesses face a lot of operating issues. Is that critical? Can't financial engineering turn investor profits without really solving the more fundamental corporate value concerns?

Not any more. All of the financial performance delivered by financial engineering and presentation during the past two decades was well and truly vaporized by the Great Worldwide Meltdown. Didn't work. The system that DOES deliver value and still survives is a deceptively simple equation:

EFFICIENCY = PROFIT = QUALITY

They're all connected; you don't get any of them unless you get all of them. And the way you get them is through effective management of value. This requires a broad-spectrum effort focused on the multiple areas which drive business efficiency. We'll look at the specific problems in a bit more detail as we examine globally competitive solutions. This will involve a batch of processes we haven't seen in many businesses recently.

THE SPECIALIST PROBLEM

There's a major factor that keeps us from addressing this seemingly-simple efficiency equation. It's major because it's driven managerial staffing for the past quarter-century. This is the bias toward specialization, a quirk that's created a generation of management problems culminating in the Great Worldwide Meltdown.

Professional firms – law firms and public accounting practices – train most executive candidates, and those firms find specialization a valuable management tool. If they're large firms and have lots of specialists, they'll find lots of customers who need something obscure where – surprise!

17

– the firm just happens to have a world expert. The world experts stick with their employee positions because the world-class skill set isn't all that transferable: the average business needs something that esoteric only rarely, so only a large professional firm has enough work to keep them fully occupied and low enough labor costs to make a profit.

This works out for the partners in these firms, but creates issues when the experts decide to step up and run companies. Specialized skills don't work worth a damn in corporate management.

Specialists aren't good executives. They aren't effective at making money. Specialists are a fine resource, and there are certainly technological and regulatory areas where specialized expertise is necessary – but management isn't one of them. This is a problem, since the majority of U.S. executives move from specialist positions (primarily accounting or legal) where they're experts to C-level roles where the skill set that has made them successful suddenly works against them.Remember the Peter Principle: everyone gets promoted to the level of their incompetence? The highly-focused skills encouraged in Big Four accounting firms and law firms, in management consultancies and in much of the graduate curricula don't build a sound base for the specialty technician to move from esoteric projects to driving an organization.

There are many intelligent and talented people in specialist roles. Their failure in business leadership isn't due to greed, incompetence, venality, or any of the usual suspects.It's due to something far more insidious: to the nature of their skills and training when applied to the wide-ranging problems confronting top leadership. It's human nature; the reflex reaction that the new problem is best solved by the tool you've always used successfully (i.e., the really specialized skill) rather than the tool that best addresses the problem. This tunnel vision, combined with a lack of broad-based skills that must be acquired on the fly when the specialist steps up to the big chair, creates a formidable barrier to success.

THE "WHOLE PROBLEM" PROBLEM

One aspect where specialists are particularly weak is a critical skill: seeing the whole problem. We see this skill driving business excellence all the damn time.

Apple has been a stellar example during the past decade: the triumph of something like the iPod wasn't technological (the Diamond Rio and other first generation players addressed all the hardware issues) or even world-class product design, but of seeing the problem in terms of consumer desires rather than esoteric knowledge.

A customer doesn't want an MP3 player. They don't specifically want a control wheel or even a sleek and aesthetic case. They want to get the music they want, when they want it, in as simple-to-use a format as possible. The combination of device (the iPod itself) and content (an iTunes Web site with huge selection in an inexpensive and easily-operated format) solved the problem – a solution which was driven by understanding of the whole customer problem, not of particular skills.

This is an extension of Jobs' earlier mass market introduction of the graphic user interface with the Macintosh, which recognized that mass acceptance of desktop computing required both desktop ease and power (which they got from any number of sources) and a simple, intuitive use (which Jobs gave them through the graphic metaphors he borrowed/ripped off from Xerox). The iPhone is the latest extension of the same philosophy: my customer wants to carry less small appliances around with them and have still better ergonomics, so I design a phone that gives them all of the above.

Where's the problem? Recent business history shows the value of management aimed at solving the whole problem, not creating a patchwork quilt of savants operating in organizational silos. We're ass-deep in savants, and real short of people focused on value and solving customer problems.

Specialists tend to look at their piece of the process (the esoteric chunks where they're so competent) rather than the entire problem-solving recipe. The preparation of most CEOs sends them looking for "safe" experts instead of people with a larger vision who see the overall problems and processes that drive value. It's perhaps no accident that both incarnations of Apple (and Pixar) were driven by Steve Jobs, a non-specialist outsider, albeit a talented one, who has no certifications and never made it through college. (Bill Gates, another high achiever, has the same credentials; the same's true of Steven Spielberg and Richard Branson ...)

SO WHERE'S OUR MID-SIZED COMPANY EXECUTIVE?

He's looking for two things: concepts he can use to solve problems and create new opportunities, and tools he can use to execute. As a management professional, he wants to create corporate value.

This is more complicated than application of a Value at Risk formula to situations it was never meant to address, as we've seen in recent events. It requires hands-on management of the processes, systems and assets creating value by a management that's looking at the whole problem. The tools used by that management are the methods that will make your company globally competitive. It's time to look a bit deeper at the concepts and tools that are needed.

III
SOME VALUE-DRIVING CONCEPTS

Creating value requires us to set the stage. We can't accomplish the extraordinary if we're thinking conventionally. This becomes more true than ever in a situation such as we face now, where markets, technologies and the world economy are shifting continually.With this in mind, let's think about some issues that will shape our development of concepts and tools for mid-sized company success.

THERE'S NO SUCH THING AS A NATIONAL COMPANY

Much has been said about product regulation barriers in Europe; about predatory pricing by the Chinese and "dumping" by the Japanese, and selective patent enforcement throughout Asia. On the other side of the Atlantic, much has also been said about dumping of food products – and of poor quality or unhygienic food products – by the United States. Nations see this in national terms: one country's businesses against the other guy's.This misses the nature of modern manufacturing.

What's an "American business?" Food products usually come from a single location. But most products don't have this limitation. I recently worked on a consumer electronics peripheral where a British-patented noise reduction technology was built into a chip manufactured at a Palo Alto foundry and included in a device fabricated in Shenzhen that was sold in the Middle East and South America.

What nation benefits from this set of international transactions? The actual company which sold the device was American, but how many workers gained from its product? On the other hand, the company's U.S. shareholders certainly benefited, and their profits helped strengthen U.S. consumer markets.

In the last century there was much discussion of the potential benefits from vertical integration, of a corporation controlling every step of its production and sales process. What we're seeing now is the competitive power of vertical DIS-integration, where every element of the company's process is world class, or it's outsourced to another source that is.

Much global competition operates beyond the grasp of any single nation-state – which may be the reason that so many government types find international trade a threatening concept. But many U.S. entrepreneurs don't find global manufacturing threatening at all: it allows them to create products and build businesses that would never exist if the fabrication had to take place in American plants at American labor prices and under American regulatory restrictions. This is a more complicated issue than the headlines would suggest.

This is an opportunity for the executive in a mid-sized company. They can introduce new products faster while eliminating the need for expensive factories and production lines. In a world where product lifecycles are decreasing, this is attractive.

THERE'S NO "FORCE OF HISTORY"
That Limits Companies in "Declining Countries" Such as the U.S.

You see this myth everywhere. In large parts of Europe and Asia, people believe a variant that I call "Your turn's coming!" The rationale behind these beliefs is that America is an old, decadent power which will be inevitably overthrown – in corporate battlefields or otherwise – by younger and more aggressive powers who will rise and break the shackles of bloated market imperialism. This is a rationale which assumes that businesses are "national" rather than driven by shareholder interests. As we saw above, that's not true. And it conveniently overlooks Americans' innovative leadership in fields from nanotechnology to fashion design. It also assumes that entrepreneurship and executive leadership are driven by governmental-political initiatives, a concept where the jury's still out.

The weird thing about this is that I run into this concept all the time IN AMERICA. Otherwise intelligent people actually believe that we're doomed to be overrun by the unstoppable foreign business hordes.Baloney!

Any "Force of History" isn't aimed solely at the U.S., and a "Force of Management Stupidity" may be far more decisive in business survival. Yet the concept of "American decadence" lies on. These beliefs pop up regularly, from Paris to Jeddah to Ho Chi Minh City, without any serious evidence to back them up.

The death of America, to paraphrase Mark Twain, has been greatly exaggerated.

NATIONS CAN'T HELP THEIR CITIZENS COMPETE

This is a hot issue for fans of Detroit iron, and it's a cautionary tale. Remember Japan's commitment to the "Fifth Generation Computing" that was going to dominate information technology and send Microsoft and Oracle to the minor leagues? Didn't happen.

Remember Malaysia's drive to make itself the electronics manufacturing center of Southeast Asia? That didn't happen, either. While we're at it, we can remember legends of King Canute commanding the tide to stop – which set the management standard used ever since by government subsidy boondoggles ranging from the Fifth Generation and GM to Airbus.

Governments can throw their national balance sheet at such initiatives. But, as we saw when George Soros led the short sales that broke British pound, they can't stand up against a market with the bit in its teeth. Government failures have been frequent, but their successes limited (a sobering thought, considering the current wave of multi-billion dollar bailouts). Government help also comes with government input. Since governments operate by fiat (and Fiat, in the case of the Chrysler bailout) rather than market demand, this makes their input risky for the recipient.

Those of us who've manufactured in the PRC have seen this first-hand. Some segments of PRC manufacturing still have management techniques left over from Joe Stalin and the Five Year Plans. They tell their customers what should be bought and what it should look like, proclaiming their "industry and engineering expertise" to anyone who will listen. This is fine when the government picks up the check – but if the customer listens, they often end up footing the bill in the form of excess inventory and products that don't meet consumer taste.

Corporate managers need to view this trend with skepticism. Today's subsidy is tomorrow's iron shackle, as executives from Jamie Dimon to Lloyd Blankfein have verified recently.

"COOL" ISN'T A COOL STRATEGY

A surprising number of young companies still believe in magic; they're sure that their people are so much smarter and more creative and hipper than everyone else's that they'll succeed and keep on succeeding. Apparently, these people never heard of Joy's Law.

Bill Joy, one of the founders of Sun Micro (a case study of the rise and fall of techno-hipsters in its own right), set out a dictum which has proved itself with depressing regularity:

"The best people always work for your competitor"

You can't hire all the smart guys. Microsoft spent several hundred million dollars trying in the late Nineties, when Nathan Mhyrvold was throwing big contracts to every hot researcher in the Solar System. Didn't work. It never does.

You can't hire all the cool guys. Cool guys try to avoid critical mass, and the truly cool will avoid a concentration that would just have them sink into spearcarrier roles in the crowd.

Cool also has a short shelf life. Today's hipster is tomorrow's boring loser left in the dust by the onward progress of style, fashion and success du jour. And today's hipster whose product has been knocked off by a low cost cloner sees the dust even more quickly, since cool doesn't often survive a few containers of half price, bad quality fakes.

COMPANIES CAN'T STAY STATIC

Many bright and personable executives are still undone by the most deadly belief in modern business, the insidious belief that:

THEN = NOW

It doesn't. A 2006 Accenture study of the Russell 3000 over fifteen years ("Do Investors Believe in Sustainable Competitive and Strategic Advantage?") suggested that, as Michael Porter predicted, competitive advantage shrinks over time and excess growth returns are competed away over time. Product lifecycles shrink. Technologies become obsolete. The skills of today's workforce become the obsolete crafts of metaphorical phrenologists and whalebone corset manufacturers of the 21st century.

BUSINESS CAN'T BE TOTALLY REGULATED

Sarbanes-Oxley didn't protect a single shareholder in the Great Worldwide Meltdown. The U.K's Financial Services Authority, created in 1997 to administer the sort of comprehensive oversight that so many now favor for the U.S., still allowed what Prime Minister Gordon Brown referred to as "irresponsible risk taking, incompetent risk management, and inadequate due diligence" and required massive financial intervention and support by the Crown. Ditto the rest of Europe, and the PRC.

The collapse was due to issues that are much harder to regulate, notably the unforeseen failure of the Value at Risk formula (a commonly-used tool for analyzing risk exposure in banks and investment funds).Regulations prescribe and enforce the management of problems by dictating what actions can (and can't) be taken. This will only work if you understand the situation you're regulating – and fails when you don't.

"Enforce" is a tricky component in that previous sentence. Money votes with its feet. When a regulator becomes hostile enough, money packs up its troubles in its old kit bag and goes somewhere that isn't quite as troubling.

HOW DO THESE CONCEPTS HELP US MANAGE?

It's hard to be efficient when you're sorting black cats in coal cellars at midnight. It's also hard to be efficient when you're applying solutions that are designed for a world that doesn't exist. Understanding reality's more useful than ignoring it.

There's something in most people – and certainly in most managers – that longs for tradition, that believes that the old ways are best.Experts can make better decisions than we can, and we have to trust them.

That something causes people to sign up with fast-talking Bernie Madoff because he's a known Wall Street leader. It causes entrepreneurs who should know better to believe that a GAAP financial statement always gives them a true picture of their company's financial condition. It causes widows and orphans (to say nothing of middle class wage earners) to place their retirement investments in the hands of banks that are busily buying and selling credit default swaps that neither they nor anyone else can accurately value.

Trust is an expensive hobby. Mythologies need to stay on the history bookshelf. Executives who'll win by creating value will be those who can work without them.

IV
WHY CAN'T I BE CERTAIN?

Why can't we trust the stuff that's worked for our most successful companies? A personal example may illustrate the issue.

When I was young, I was a science fiction junkie. One of the most thought-provoking of the science fiction tomes with which I whiled away my antisocial and pathetically awkward pre-adolescence was a well-known trilogy by Isaac Asimov, *Foundation*. For those who missed out, this is a "future history" based on a (yet undiscovered) set of forecasting tools called "psychohistory" which could be used to accurately project events decades before they happened.

It's an old idea. French mathematician Pierre-Simon Laplace first raised the concept in the early nineteenth century, and it recurred in Bertrand Russell's *Principia Mathematica* and in David Hilbert's famous Twenty-Three Questions in the early twentieth century.

This theme recurs like malaria in science fiction: in addition to Asimov, another SF writer named "Doc" Smith wrote the "Lens" series, which featured aliens with such great stochastic modeling skills that they could calculate the fall of hairs from the head of a barbershop patron five years in the future.Get the right equations and you can plan ANYTHING at any desired level of detail.The concept was the same in all cases: with enough input and good enough algorithms, a totally accurate prediction should be possible.)

Of course, there was another guy from the same period in history as Asimov and Doc Smith who believed in the ability to perfectly forecast the future: a fellow named Josef Stalin. He thought you could write five year plans and make them work out exactly. His forecasts proved to be more fiction than science, as you can tell since the country he ran with those equations, the Soviet Union, is now as non-existent as the Foundation. Various whiz kids and CEOs had similar track records, and the Manhattan Fund, portfolio insurance, derivatives and the career of Richard Fuld ain't what they used to be.

Trust – whether of leaders, certifications, or our own analyses – is more risky than Vegas, where you visit knowing that the odds are against you and you'll lose money. Belief is expensive, even when it's belief in the Best and the Brightest.

WE HAVE NOTHING TO FEAR BUT FEAR ITSELF
– But Fear Of The Unknown Is Pretty Damn Scary

How could all our leaders and experts be so damn wrong? The answer is, EVERYBODY'S wrong all the time – but the rest of us realize it and don't claim infallibility. Why do we flock to those claiming they never make a mistake?

Behavioral psychology is having something of a Renaissance these days, particularly among business types who are applying it to corporate management.

Two of the fantastic, velvet rope, super-stylish ultratrendies in this area are Amos Tversky and Daniel Kahneman, who've found some interesting things about the ways people make decisions. In Tversky and Kahneman's studies, the way we make decisions is primarily driven by galloping, quivering fear: potential threats are weighted much more heavily in our brains than possible gains. This affects what we see and how we look for it. There are biases built into the core of our risk analytic processes: the functioning of our brains.

If our analytic weighting of threats, rewards and risk is off, we're going to make decisions based on twitching synapses rather than reality. Those reflexes our cave ancestors developed fleeing sabertooths and giant ground sloths aren't useful when evaluating new product opportunities.

We get uncomfortable when we see potential threats. One of the best ways to avoid this discomfort is to not look very hard. When we trust someone or some established solution, we have confidence in what the trusted person will do and the solution will create. So we like standards; we like certifications, and we like established industry wisdom.

If only we knew what any of those things really meant.

DEFINING THINGS

The problem's deeper than a few bad reflexes. We don't really know what we're talking about because we CAN'T.

Certainty – in the business world or anywhere else – is limited by the nature of reality. "There are things that mankind was not meant to know," as Bela Lugosi reminds us in *The Invisible Ray*. But what ol' Drac left out from his Transylvanian-accented dissertation was the fact that mankind wasn't meant to know them due to the structure of the Universe itself.

A few basic math and physics concepts are in order:

A fellow named Sir Karl Popper is famed for a much-validated analysis of the nature of reality. It's known as The Falsity Principle, and it goes like this:

In the real world there are any number of reasons why any event could take place, since real events are complex and take place in even more complex environments filled with unnoticed variables that we can't even begin to factor into a calculation. As a result, the fact that something took place doesn't really prove anything. We don't know WHY it took place. The only time that an event proves something is when you predicted it and it DOESN'T take place: then you've proved your prediction model is wrong.

A large number of real world risk-takers from George Soros to Nassim Taleb to numerous turnaround executives have made zillions from applying Popper's concepts to investment. They work. So we know when we're wrong, not when we're right.

Why? Let's consider the real blockbuster highlights of math and information theory of the last century that affect everything around us, and think of what they're telling us. I'd nominate the following:

1. Einstein's Special and General Theories of Relativity demonstrated that objects don't have an absolute location in space or time. They're located RELATIVE to other phenomena.

    Einstein says there's no absolute location or speed. There isn't a single, measurable reality – it all depends on where you are, how fast you're moving, where other things are, and how fast they're moving. And the Universe itself is moving, which means everything is rattling around in ways that distort any absolute evaluation. Measurements are a moving target (literally).

2.   Schrödinger, Heisenberg, and the quantum mechanics physicists showed there are limits to what can EVER be learned about a particular electron: its exact location can be known at a given time, or its precise momentum at a given time, but never both at the same instant. This isn't an issue of measure; this is an issue of what's possible. You can't know everything about a particular unit of matter – which is going to make it difficult to predict the relations between large numbers of unpredictable units of matter. Admittedly, most of us operate in larger work areas than a single electron – but the implications hold true for larger groups of objects, which are (after all) composed of large numbers of these non-specific quantum objects.

3.   The great mathematician David Hilbert once proposed a contest (which everyone of his time thought would be pretty easy) to demonstrate that mathematics was internally consistent and could therefore be applied just as Laplace predicted. No problem.

But then another mathematician and all-around odd guy named Kurt Gödel showed that there are mathematical issues which can't be proved even though we're sure they're "true." Still another mathematician/ gearhead named Gregory Chaitin followed this up by extending Gödel's work to prove that there are more of these things than there are things which CAN be proved. Limits to knowledge aren't a matter of trying harder to finding data – they're structural.

4.   During World War Two, a strange but brilliant British MI6 codebreaker named Alan Turing (breakthrough math and personal oddness travel pretty closely, which may say something we'd probably rather ignore about the nature of reality ...) then demonstrated a couple of other related issues through an analysis of what he called the "Halting Problem." Using a very adaptable version of computer programming, he demonstrated that:

a. Anything in the universe can be simulated by a sufficiently complex logical-mathematical model, and

b. Once that happens, the results of that model-thing's operation still can't be predicted with total accuracy, even if you made another model using the identical components.

This leaves us with a basic conclusion:

THERE'S A LOT OF STUFF
WE'RE NEVER GONNA KNOW

This isn't esoteric philosophy, either. It's all around us; we've just been trained to pay no attention.

Let's look at some high school algebra to consider how basic the limits of math really are. We've all heard people (mostly non-mathematicians, but people) going on about "mathematical precision." With that in mind, think about a simple calculation:

a. One-third can be written as either 1/3 or .33 ...

b. Let's let "x" equal three-thirds, or .99 ... in mathematical notation

c. In that case, "10x" equals 9.99 ... (which is 10 times .99 ...)

d. "9x" should then equal "10x" minus "x," or 9.99 ... minus .99 ...

e. Therefore, "9x" equals 9, and "x" equals 1. Of course, we started out noting that "x" equals .99 ...

We've now got "x" equal to both:

1. a whole ("1"), and

2. part of a whole (".99 ...")

And this isn't the only time where common math does weird stuff when we let it. Take that old favorite derived by math legend Georg Cantor in the 19th century:

$$\infty \times \infty = \infty$$

Infinity times infinity equals infinity. The thing multiplied times itself (or added to itself, in this case) equals itself. This goes well with that old high school favorite:

$$0 \times 0 = 0$$

Zero times zero equals zero. So how precise is "mathematical precision," anyway?

KING'S X

There have been any number of articles and books written about paradox and ambiguity in mathematics. Most of them have very poor dialog and characterization, but they make an important and well-recognized point: there are limits to the "precision" of math itself.

So why doesn't the subject come up in corporate operations or finance? Why is "King's X" declared on well-accepted math the minute we move from the general structure of mathematics to company-specific accounting?

Corporate groups work with technical tools, but they frequently don't think about what the tools really are. And (dirty little managerial secret revealed here) most of those folks who made it through MBA programs and accounting certification did it without REALLY having much beyond four function math (i.e., addition, subtraction, multiplication and division) – they get nervous when you pop the hood on the math stuff and take a look at the details.

But, as we saw in the Great Worldwide Meltdown and its related contraction of borrowing lines, understanding the system isn't academic. Assuming balance sheet numbers are steady-state when they're dependent on actions of reserve relief, mark to market (or derivative markets, currency markets, tranche risk in derivatives pricing, or market perceptions – take your pick) is a short path to corporate suicide.

It's relatively easy to spot the common things that happen, so (in the corporate version of looking for your lost keys under the nearest streetlight because that's where you can see) most management spends a lot of time looking at the common stuff. This is a great way to miss the important stuff, which may not be as obvious as you assume:

Let's examine the following graph:

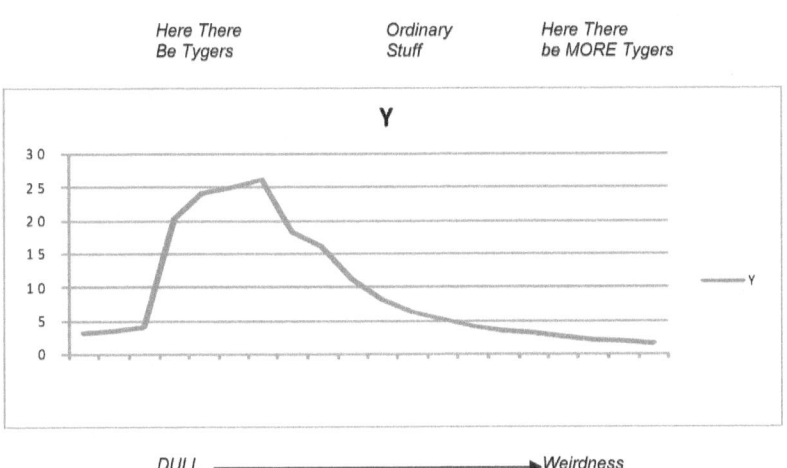

This is one of those "fat tail" distribution curves that have been written about lately. Like all too many of us, it consists of a thick center with narrow, elongated extremities. That big center is where the common stuff happens, and it's pretty plain vanilla. Predictable. The ends are where the weird stuff happens, where things get very good or very bad.Or very strange.They're the parts of the old maps labeled "Here There be Tygers,"

and filled with skulls and crossbones, treasure caves, and three-headed dragons.

Classic management spends all its time looking at the fat middle.

This is a problem, as economists and mathematicians such as Benoit Mandelbrot and Riccardo Rebonato have been saying for years. A lot of modern business is taking place in those end zone, "Here There Be Tygers" regions. Preserving your intellectual comfort by only looking at the stuff in the safe, comfortable middle means risking a lot of your business.

Many underpinnings of modern finance, notably the Black-Scholes model, the Li "Gaussian copula" equations used to price the various tranches of bond portfolios, and Value at Risk, all assume that financial risk is distributed over a Gaussian "bell curve" (which is probably wrong, and which means that - if the curve should be fat-tailed - VaR, the Li equation and Black-Scholes won't give the right answers). Further, they assume that, once I've got a curve with so many data points that the whole curve is highly predictable, then *each piece of the curve is predictable with equal accuracy* (which is wrong and which makes no sense).

Some of the models used in plain ol' bank management (let alone all that multi-order derivative stuff) are dealing with events that might have happened once since the fall of Rome – do you really think that we've got enough data to predict those end pieces of the curve worth a damn? I don't: the data points at the Six Sigma ends of that fat tail are NOT as frequent as those in the entire curve; they aren't very frequent at all.And if the curve slope is even a little different than we think it is, that difference will be massively magnified out at the ends of the curve where things get strange. The same ends of the curve that affect things like default rates in mortgage swaps and multi-order derivative instruments.

A basic overlooked law of the Universe: the fact that something works A LOT doesn't mean that it works EVERY DAMN TIME. We need a well-exercised sense of skepticism. There are few things in this world that can be totally relied upon. The truth IS out there, just like they said in the *X-Files* before it got cancelled, but it's impossible to ever see what the truth IS. Reality is structurally obscured, so using financial and accounting tools that assume total accuracy isn't a great idea.

Periodically, we recognize this. The U.S. legal system is built on standards of proof – "beyond a reasonable doubt" or "preponderance of evidence" – rather than an assumption that unassailable facts can be found. Yet many of our planning processes act as though there's an "ultimate truth," and that we'll track it down with sufficient work.

So, as managers predicting the results of our decisions, we're in trouble. Even if we could see that "ultimate truth," we couldn't apply it perfectly. You CAN'T design an infallible prediction system, though too many accounting personnel act otherwise. They assume it's fine when people are using imprecise business techniques to give a absolute and precise indication of exactly where a business allegedly is at a point in time.

That doesn't work. Reality can never be forecasted with 100% accuracy. Asimov's Foundation Trilogy isn't going to make it from the fiction shelf to the Board room; that stuff works in science fiction but not in reality.

"ULTIMATE TRUTH" ADDICTION

Lots of people love the "ultimate truth." We see this with depressing regularity in the workplace, where established damn-foolishness regularly mops the floor with intelligent quality improvement initiatives. Raise your hand if you've heard any of the following phrases in the past week:

"We've used this method for years"

"It's industry standard"

"We know what we're doing"

So sorry. We only know SOME of what we're doing, and the stuff we don't know can and will kill us unless we work to catch the errors in our ways as quickly and frequently as possible. Killing this idea of Platonic perfection and sacred truth is Ground Zero for a lot of corporate rescue projects.

LET'S GET NEGATIVE!

I'm about to say some terrible things about accounting, so I should explain myself, and tell you why I'm sounding so negative.

Some of my best friends are accountants – which isn't too surprising, since I used to work for a "Big Four" accounting firm and lecture for the CalCPA. Most accountants that I know are dedicated, intelligent professionals who sincerely want to do a good job.

If only it were that simple.

Accounting, the system, is seriously injured. What happened? Tales of frogs adapting to boiling cauldrons and roads to Hell paved with good intentions come to mind.

At its core, this problem is driven by the desire for certainty (held by the client) and the desire to be an authority (held by the accountant)."Certainty" is a strange concept when applied to accounting. When your CPA issues an audit, it's labeled as an "opinion." Not as "the Ultimate Truth." Why should the numbers in something called an "opinion" be treated as totally accurate?

Accounting and Finance drive the decisions in many companies.And, like Joe Stalin and David Hilbert, too many managers view those financial numbers as parts of a precise, totally computable system.That hasn't worked out too well for them, as we've seen with everything from Enron to the Great Worldwide Meltdown.

WHY ARE ACCOUNTANTS SAYING THOSE TERRIBLE THINGS ABOUT THEMSELVES?

You already know that I've got my doubts. But I've got company. It turns out that the accountants aren't agreed on the nature of Absolute Truth, either.We can see this in the SEC's proposed shift from Generally Accepted Accounting Principles ("GAAP") to International Financial Records Standards ("IFRS").

This is a much less boring topic than it appears. (Didn't set the bar very high, did I?) The issues behind the rejection of GAAP – the system on which U.S. financial operations and the whole certified public accounting apparatus have been built over the last half century – and the adoption of a new system controlled outside of the U.S. accounting establishment tell us useful things about the certainty of financial numbers, the reliability of accounting experts, and the use of numerical analysis in management. Most of these issues will still be in the center of financial management after GAAP's only a memory.

GAAP OR GAP?

Christopher Cox, the former head of the Securities and Exchange Commission, surfaced the issue when he noted that one of his primary goals was to draw up plans for moving accounting standards for the SEC-required financial reporting by public companies from the current GAAP standards to the European (IFRS) standards by the end of 2008. This was followed up by a draft recommendation (circulated for public comment before final adoption) that would scrap GAAP by 2014 and converge U.S. standards with IFRS. More recently, the new head of the SEC, Mary Schapiro, stated "I will take a deep breath and will not necessarily feel bound by the existing roadmap that is out there for comment," further clouding an already murky issue.

To the uninitiated, this sounds pretty screwed up. This is because it really IS screwed up. And the reasoning that produced the current confusion is quite relevant to our consideration of Cargo Cults, value, global competition, and effective management processes.

The Cult of GAAP accounting has been quite useful in company politics.

Banks have always had a large vote in business financial operations, and GAAP has been designed for the purpose of loan underwriting, not business operation. They're pushing GAAP. Add the generation of financial executives who grew up inside "Big Four" accounting firms (which have always been focused on GAAP accounting because it's the basis for the audits their firms sell, and which gave them the pedigree to land those top jobs), and you've got a big lobby for the status quo.

The fact it doesn't do anything for executives when they're building value is incidental.

There's also the "Masters of the Universe" issue. Many finance executives are attracted to the glamour and excitement of mergers and acquisitions, which – being governed by financing considerations – are also driven by GAAP issues. The result is a generation of finance executives who consider management accounting and costing – the tools which guide business operations – as something boring and clerical and beneath them.

The reasons for status quo worship are as emotional as analytic. Most accountants are real uncomfortable with the ambiguity found in actual management accounting – just like the rest of us – and prefer the alleged "certainties" of GAAP. They also found that proclaiming GAAP as the one "truth" makes chief financial officers the Keepers of Truth and gives them greater political power within the organization. (As a former CFO, I can certainly recognize the attractiveness of the approach ...)

Why is there pressure to change their tune?

ADVENTURES IN RECENT GAAP FINANCIALS

An example. Let's look at the Bear Stearns crisis, when one of America's best-known investment banks went down in flames after its subprime loan exposure turned out to be more than advertised. In particular, let's remember that on November 30th before the March meltdown, Bear's "Big Four" auditors (Deloitte Touche, for those who hold a grudge) issued a clean opinion showing Bear with a net worth of $11.7 billion, when four months later it turned out the valuation was really NOTHING.

What did that tell us about the value of GAAP and its application? Note that Deloitte wasn't charged with shoddy work or misrepresentation or anything else regarding Bear Stearns – the legal process assumed that the vagaries of markets and imprecision of processes are such that an $11 billion swing in four months was a legitimate expectation for GAAP. "Truth" apparently runs plus or minus $11 billion.

The Bear Stearns audit opinion wasn't a fluke. Before AIG was bailed out the amount that was needed went up by $45 billion in three days and kept going from there. How accurate were their statements? When do we get to the "absolute truth" of financial statement numbers, in banking or in management?

ACCOUNTING PRINCIPLES – OR RITUALS?

Long ago when dinosaurs ruled the earth and I worked for a "Big Four" accounting firm – actually, they were "Big Six" firms at that remote point in history – finance was driven by a concept called "principles-based accounting." Under this approach, the accountant built a financial statement that reflected underlying concepts: matching of assets with their associated liabilities, depreciation schedules matching the useful life of the item being depreciated, etc.

Some time after my tenure in public accounting firms, the Financial Accounting Standards Board (the "FASB," as it's known in the jargon-happy depths of the accounting profession), which is the governing body that decides what is and is not included in the rules governing Generally Accepted Accounting Principles, decided to move from this approach to something called "rules-based accounting" which – as you'd figure from the name – built the financial statement using specific rules and procedures. The cookbook approach to corporate finance. The theory here was that you don't really know what someone is doing when they're applying principles and judgment, but you know exactly what happened when they're applying specified rules.

This is one of those concepts that sounds better than it works out in practice.

Back in the era of principles-based accounting, there were thirty-something concepts – cleverly called "FAS" (from "financial accounting standards"; they were named by accountants, not poets) – which described the principles being applied. These concepts were relatively straightforward. With rules-based accounting, there are now over two hundred FAS standards, and many of them are as complex, poorly articulated and esoteric as you'd expect from an extremely bureaucratic system drafted by a bunch of people who went into accounting in college because they were lousy writers and feared law school.

Principles-based accounting insisted that an accountant couldn't produce statements that obviously didn't reflect the real situation, whether they'd been created following the standard rules or not. Rules-based accounting doesn't have that limit.

A real world example, you say?

Option accounting is an issue which FASB claims is a victory. They finally got a rule for recognizing costs for options. The issue of whether that rule accurately shows the value impact of those options is a classic illustration of the problem with rules as a measure of value. How did they solve the problem of reflecting the dilution to per-share earnings when options are exercised?

They used a fixed rule. Accounting practice went from ignoring the problem (showing nothing for options costs) to the current approach required under FAS123r, which sets required reserves based on financial models (the

Black-Scholes approach, which has been demonstrated to overstate costs and was disavowed by one of the people who developed it in the first place, or a binomial approach that few CFOs actually understand). It then sets a mandatory charge to income for all options, in many cases whether or not they are fully vested. It's a rule, but it's not a rule that reflects reality very well.

In simple terms, we've gone from recognizing nothing for a future dilution of share earnings to recognizing dilution which may never take place – and pricing that potential dilution using financial models which can be manipulated to significantly affect the balance sheet impact. This adds share volatility while it subtracts pricing accuracy. It takes a certain talent to come up with two demonstrably misleading approaches in a row and successively build them into accounting requirements, but that's what's happened in the U.S. accounting system. Mark to market accounting, in which securities are priced to today's sale price whether or not they've defaulted and the ultimate cash flow stream has been impaired, takes a similar approach.Potential events become actual costs.

Things like this are one of the many reasons that private equity firms (i.e., people who spend a lot of time considering real value versus apparent value, since mistakes in valuation are costly when you're doing leveraged deals) spend a lot of time examining the differences in value from free cash flow multiples and the sale value of assets rather than blindly following GAAP.

WHAT'S STORED IN THAT INVENTORY?

I've been involved in mergers and acquisitions for several decades now. After all that time, I'm still waiting for some milestone events in my career.One of these will be the first time that I go through a due diligence investigation of inventory and have the same inventory valuation at the end of the process as when it started. I'm not optimistic that this will happen any time soon.

Inventory value almost always changes in due diligence, even when there's been an audit beforehand. The actual objects are different than the accounting entries. Inventory goes out of date, if you're in the food or pharmaceuticals industries. Products become obsolete. Inventory gets lost or broken, if you're in ANY industry. Inventory goes out of fashion and has to be liquidated for insignificant fractions of its alleged book value. Inventory gets stolen by the warehouse staff, and the thefts aren't discovered until months later. I did one project where replacing the security cameras in the warehouse was an expected weekly cost of business because the warehouse staff all had side careers in the Mexican Mafia's corporate theft division. This created some confusion regarding what inventory existed at any point in time.

Inventory is always a part of the balance sheet. It's seldom a correctly-valued part of the balance sheet. GAAP's version of the "absolute truth" doesn't address this.

DEPRECIATION

GAAP normally assumes that assets lose value over their "useful lives." "Useful life" is defined by convention, which has a questionable relation to reality.

Software often is depreciated over three to five years – two years can be a lifetime when you're looking at code. Real property is depreciated over thirty-one years – does anyone really expect the structure to collapse into powder on the thirty-second anniversary?

And depreciation is normally made on a straight line basis; the reductions are made in equal chunks. Does that have any relation to actual funds realized if you turned around and sold the item?

IS IFRS THE ANSWER?

Now that the SEC potentially agrees with me that there are problems with GAAP (and believe me, we've only scratched the surface on that subject) is the problem solved? Will IFRS bring on the New Golden Age of Accounting?

There will be some benefits from IFRS (if Schapiro lets it happen):

- It's a bit simpler, which means there will be less confusion about what the standard's trying to accomplish.
- It's principles-based: a BIG gain if it forces people to issue statements that make some sense rather than ones that simply follow orders (as is the case with GAAP)
- It will make consolidation of multinational businesses easier, since there won't be translation issues from one set of standard to another.
- As a multinational standard, it will be harder for special interests to change and manipulate.

But this is going to be a painful issue for U.S. companies during the transition process. More confusion; less certainty. The process – moving every element of the general ledger from GAAP to IFRS conventions – will require a transition of every factor in the Chart of Accounts, particularly in understanding the re-definition that's being imposed on every financial data element that's used in corporate management. Companies must map historical data over from GAAP to IFRS and make sure that corporate managers who are using the information understand what just happened. Equally important, executives will have to make their corporate partners – banks, joint venture allies, customers, and all the rest – understand what just happened. This will take time and thought, and is an issue that's being largely ignored by the managements we've questioned about it. This isn't a recipe for certainty.

Intellectual property is a major facet of modern corporate value. (The rise in share price to book ratios over the past decade on U.S. exchanges – from three times to six times – is a concrete illustration of the growth in intangibles as a component of total share value.) Neither GAAP nor IFRS have compelling methods of managing intangible assets or reflecting them in accounting or financial data.

Why is this so difficult? A core problem comes from the (understandable) desire for simple presentation in financial statements. The desire to make the statements stand alone as single pages, without forcing users to refer to the footnotes describing how they were put together, seems attractive. It's a nice idea – but overly simple statements result in overly simple-minded user analyses when they're considering complex situations. Putting more information specifically in the statement footnotes would make the statements more useful and the assumptions baked into them more evident. Placing contingent items on the balance sheet (as happens with options) just makes the statement less functional.

DOES EXPERT CERTIFICATION WORK?

The short answer is: how did you enjoy the Great Worldwide Meltdown, and how much did audit requirements, GAAP, bank regulation, Sarbanes-Oxley, and SEC/FASB oversight keep things on an even keel?

The long answer is: any system where the certifiers are paid by people who use their certified opinion to sell the alleged value and solvency of an investment (or a loan, or whatever) to someone else has an insoluble conflict of interests.

Accounting firm partners – or bond rating agencies, who committed far more preposterous acts in the name of "client service" than any accountant ever conceived – get partnership shares and other tangible rewards NOW for pushing the edge of the envelope, and then move on to manage firms that pay lobbyists (or, in the case of Big Four accounting firms, have an incestuously-close relationship with the staff of the FASB who largely come from and return to those firms). It works great for the certifiers, but not so hot for those using the opinion.

At this point, anyone who would trust a certification produced by this process would believe in the Easter Bunny, Perez Hilton, UFOs, astrology, and the psychic powers of their pets.

Oh yeah, that includes most of the population of the United States ...

SOCIETE GENERALE

We've all heard "garbage in equals garbage out".It's easier to keep the garbage out when someone keeps an eye on the garbage can. This applies to corporate records as well as other types of garbage.

A modern parable. At the beginning of 2008, we had an interesting illustration of what can slide through the records in a modern company. This was the infamous Societe Generale meltdown: a Gallic, Moliere-style comedy of manners where a $70,000 a year junior trader somehow got enough slack from his pompous, bureaucratic superiors to run up $7.2 billion in losses through his attempts to Show the Big Boys that he was a Player. But nobody was laughing in France, where all of this happened.

We should restrain our chuckles as well, since this could've happened quite easily in U.S. institutions. Societe Generale was recognized as an industry leader in computerized trading controls and management, and had just been recognized as "Equity Derivatives House of the Year" by *Risk* magazine, in recognition of its superior systems and controls, on January 2008 when the fiasco surfaced. The details don't fill one with comfort:

- A junior trader was able to place $73 billion in unauthorized positions without anyone following the lead of Butch Cassidy and the Sundance Kid and asking "who is this guy"?

- While Societe Generale initially spoke of the rogue trader, Jerome Kerviel, as a master hacker, the methods he used were laughably simple. Kerviel managed the accounting entries for his own book of business. He already knew when he'd be audited by the bank's internal auditors, since they operated on a predictable schedule he'd learned when working in Societe Generale's back office. Before the audit, he'd go into the vaunted system and enter a batch of fake trades using authorization codes he'd gotten from shoulder-surfing his supervisors. When there were questions, he'd tell them "I'll sort it out" and come back with a bunch of fake e-mails from nonexistent trading partners that allegedly documented counterbalancing trades. Of course, no one in the bank worked up the interest to call the alleged e-mailers to confirm.

- Between June 2005 and the detonation in January 2008, there were 75 instances where Kerviel's weird trades triggered alerts in the bank's system, but no one pressed hard enough to confirm there was a problem.

- For those who are taking notes, Societe Generale is traded on U.S. securities exchanges, which means that it was and is subject to the allegedly investor-protecting provisions of Sarbanes-Oxley. Worked pretty well, didn't they?

- Kerviel never took vacations. Anyone who's worked on forensic accounting/"fraudit" (fraud audit) projects will recognize this as a classic behavior pattern of embezzlers worried that someone will uncover their baloney if they ever leave the office. Nobody noticed.

- Here's some of Kerviel's trading balance information:

Summer 2005 He made 500,000 euros

February 2007 He made 28 million euros

June 2007 His net losses totaled 2.2 billion euros

July 2007 His position turned around and he was net positive for 500 million euros

December 2007 He's got a net gain of 1.4 billion euros

January 2008 His position falls apart and he's got a net loss of 1.5 billion euros

All of this was wallpapered over with some fake entries and a few forged e-mails. Their auditors apparently missed multi-billion euro swings in gain and loss over a two-year period.

This interesting, since Societe Generale's trades were cleared through the (Deutsche Bank's) Eurex clearing house, whose IRIS clearing system offers Web-accessible daily risk management reports, market risk assessments on 15-minute intervals, calculations of worst case scenarios by account, and numerous other data-driven risk assessment and internal controls tools. Apparently no one wanted to go to the work of testing the book entries against independent data sources.

- Societe Generale's back office noted questions about Kerviel's trading as early as April 2007. Eurex, on its own initiative, contacted Societe Generale about Kerviel's trades in November 2007. The issue didn't get serious until Kerviel inadvertently set up one of his fake counterbalancing trades using a new client and the back office made routine calls to check the alleged client's creditworthiness for such large trades.

The upshot? A risk exposure which at one point exceeded 50 billion euros. The lesson about award-winning systems and state-of-the-art internal controls? Priceless.

U.S. corporations are committing huge amounts of resources to Sarbanes-Oxley dictated internal controls initiatives that proved just as porous as Societe Generale's award-winning internal controls package in the Great Worldwide Meltdown. SoX failed – and it diverted resources away from more effective initiatives.

The reporting problems that failed us aren't insoluble. You don't need complex procedures to understand that excluding billions of dollars in liabilities from a financial statement is misrepresentation – you simply need common sense and a minimal appreciation of the matching principle. When an Enron (to take a US equivalent) parks ten figures of liabilities off its balance sheet in a special purpose entity named after a Star Wars character and provides a 100% guarantee against loss, you don't have to be Obi-Wan Kenobi to figure that this isn't an accurate snapshot of company value – it's science fiction.

WHAT ARE ALTERNATIVES?

About now, you're possibly thinking "These certifying people are real idiots!" They're not.

The certifiers of Societe Generale financial statements – or the agencies who certify AAA-rated collateralized debt swaps manufactured out of the BBB tranche of mortgage pools, or who certified Bear Sterns statements or whatever – aren't idiots. They're charlatans, which is a different issue entirely. The idiots are the folks who trust them. You should avoid being one of them.

Now, most certifying specialists aren't frauds; most of them are dedicated and skilled enough.But how do you separate the sheep from the goats when they've all got the same certificate? The professions have spent so many decades convincing us that any certificate holder is equally qualified that now it's supposedly risky to assume they're ever wrong, no matter what the situation is that they're certifying. The certificate qualifies any of them to audit Bear Stearns, certify CDOs or whatever they've got the nerve to sign off.

Certification, by itself, isn't enough.

Remember our snappy Baudelaire quote? "To live outside the law, you must be honest"? If you can't manage honesty, you CAN at least count your change, which is the idea behind that time-honored concept in merger and acquisitions known as "due diligence" which we mentioned earlier. Due diligence is a technical way of stating that you ought to check whether you've been told the truth before you give anyone any money on the basis of an alleged "truth" someone was paid to certify. It's not necessarily limited to acquisitions, either.

That doesn't seem like a particularly difficult concept – though it's apparently too difficult for the international banking system, the SEC, and all of the folks who trust expert certification.

Ronald Reagan wasn't a classic intellectual, but he said something that's more useful in real life than a library-full of epistemology. He said "Trust, but verify." (Actually, some Russian dead guy said it first, but we'll give Ronnie credit for reminding those of us who are still breathing.) Reagan's advice remains good.

WHAT'S A LINE MANAGER SUPPOSED TO DO?

Okay, our numbers are (to be charitable) suspect. If we're a line manager, we've still got to run the company. Management must manage. So what do I suggest?

Executives can start working from basic statistics: tangible net equity, free cash flow, order book (provided the orders are covered under firm contracts).They can also use regular testing to determine when things AREN'T happening: payments are slowing down, warranty claims are increasing, etc. It doesn't take much effort to identify a few things that will show whether your assumption has problems.

And they can start developing tools to manage value and execution. How do you do that?

V
WITHOUT A NET

Your accountants and lawyers won't protect you. The bond rating agencies guarding your retirement financing have no idea what they're doing. The government is not only NOT here to help, but passes legislation ranging from Sarbanes-Oxley to ineffective fund regulations that raise the cost of compliance (i.e., lower free cash flow and, therefore, lower the value of your employer and of any stocks in your incredible shrinking retirement portfolio) without providing ANY protection against the greatest destruction of assets and value since the Great Depression.

So no one's going to protect you except YOU. How do you protect yourself?

YOU'RE RESPONSIBLE

We need to think about numbers – be they financial numbers, sales figures, operating statistics or whatever. We need to STOP using them reflexively, accepting digits on a page as absolutes without considering what they're showing us. And we've got to STOP trusting what other people are paid to tell us about numbers when they're paid by the other side of the deal – or are paid by short term CEOs to bamboozle the shareholders and the people depending on the company's long term survival.

We've got to create value. The more value we've got; the better we can deal with the slings and arrows of outrageous derivatives crises, inflationary policies or whatever.

The first great rule in building value for your business remains: don't lose the value you already have. There is a simple but powerful set of well-tested tools that will help you in this effort, all based around one of the Commandments of Effective Management:

STOP DOING DUMB STUFF

Follow this Commandment and you're a long way toward building business value.Several recent management studies, notably the work of European psychologist Dietrich Doerner on organizational problem-solving, identify a series of problem indicators which help you avoid business-threatening stupidity.I've codified them into:

**THE SEVEN EARLY
WARNING SIGNS OF DUMB STUFF**

1. ARROGANCE
2. INERTIA
3. SHORT TERM EXPEDIENCY
4. BEST CASE EXPECTATIONS
5. EXCESS LEVERAGE
6. POLITICS BEFORE PERFORMANCE
7. BAD COMMUNICATIONS

---

1. ARROGANCE
    This is shown by statements indicating the person either believes they're infallible or that they have a unique personal relationship with the Almighty which provides Divine intervention in daily business practices:

    "I know what I'm doing!"

    "I'm in control here!"

    "They'll help me out!"

    "It can't happen!"

2. INERTIA
    We all love doing what we're doing right now. And we're all great at coming up with rationalizations why our first analysis is still right, why we should stay the course, why the familiar (however dysfunctional) is more desirable than some new-fangled, untested and downright weird alternative. This never works.

    An unfortunate variant of this is something called The Sins of Edwards Deming, in which all too many cult-like devotees of otherwise good management approaches insist on Keeping the Faith, rather than measuring financial progress.There are a surprising number of Six Sigma people who grew up with this approach and still believe it (in spite of the fact that statistics tracking is at the core of the Six Sigma methodology ... Go figure.

3.   SHORT TERM EXPEDIENCY
If the thinking is ALWAYS tactical, sooner or later you'll miss a strategic issue that will kill you.

4.   BEST CASE EXPECTATIONS
If planning always uses "Goldilocks" scenarios that aren't too hot or too cold, but just right (or their equivalent in terms or timing, cost, performance, single point failure modes or whatever) – you can plan on them working out just wrong. Sooner or later, the Three Bears are gonna kick your ass.

5.   EXCESS LEVERAGE
I grew up working in leveraged buyouts. The "five times cash flow" we worked with in the Eighties has been replaced by twice that much debt, coupled with financial engineering techniques understood by no one including their developers. Most people assume this only applies to Finance, but a company that requires the one key client – or the one genius developer, or the one major product – to survive is making the same mistake. Any system that's built assuming no margin for error will eventually encounter an error requiring margin.

6.   POLITICS BEFORE PERFORMANCE
The Thousand Year Reich barely lasted ten.The Soviet Union, arguably the richest country in the world in term of natural resources, bankrupted itself. Power doesn't equal value – you can ask British Leyland, Penn Central, Bear Stearns, General Motors, ITT, International Harvester, or any of the many other businesses that substituted the fiats of corporate chieftains for sales and profits,

and squads of yes men for honest analysis. Say "no" to the Yes Men and create value – or those who do will use their balance sheets to crush your company.

7.   BAD COMMUNICATIONS
     If you don't listen to your customers, they won't tell you what they'll buy. If people don't understand what you want them to do, they won't do it. A variation of this is that well-known business phenomenon, management by adjectives ("MBA"). This gives people the illusion that they've defined a problem when all that's happened is they've talked about HOW THEY FEEL about the problem. People know your emotional state, but not what they should do about it. That's not useful – communication needs to be specific and focused on results.

There's a common theme to all of these tools: expect the unexpected. Specifically, expect the unexpected BAD NEWS.

This is a rather dyspeptic view of reality, but it's one that will keep managers from doing something they'll deeply regret (such as losing a fortune and getting fired). BAD NEWS can be limited or managed if it's expected, but will kill you if you're managing on the basis that this is the best of all possible worlds.

Good news? You don't need much preparation to manage that.

FIXING THE BAD NEWS

What do you do when you see an Early Warning Signal? You use an appropriate tool to fix things. You can recognize appropriate tools, since they've got a couple of characteristics:

Comprehensiveness:
Comprehensive tools can be used throughout the company.They don't require specialists. Companies built by specialists approach problems as a series of specialty crises. This leaves the fundamental issues – market viability, value creation, risk management – ignored in favor of a series of esoteric micro-concerns. Comprehensive tools address these basics.

Ephemeralization:
Better tools make the company simpler: they reduce the number of operations, of tools, of separate elements."Ephemeralization" is a term developed back when dinosaurs ruled the earth by my former mentor and collaborator, Buckminster Fuller (the fellow who invented the geodesic dome and a lot of the "sustainable technology" approaches that are finally getting traction as tools for ecological problems). Fuller's idea was simple.Better solutions have less mass: they focus on the minimum number of elements and the smallest amount of assets needed to resolve an issue. They edit out the things that don't directly contribute. As solutions get better, the material, financial and personnel assets used to achieve the result become less and less.

Less is more. This is becoming a major driver in business change.

Companies such as San Francisco's Pokono show us the next wave of ephemeralization in business. Pokono, the self-billed "world's largest marketplace for product plans," allows customers to license plans for furniture, jewelry, musical instruments, kitchen utensils and other products for a small fee and have Pokono fabricate (using its computer-controlled milling machines) their dream device. Once the product or part is created, Pokono ships it off to the purchaser. Look, ma – no shop floor, no inventory, no minimum orders, no sales channels or retailers. The customer selects what they want and gets it built without middlemen.

Another example. In the past five years, 3-D printing fabricators have dropped from several million dollars (the price tag of the first one I saw at BMW Designworks) to $3,600 for the open source Fab@home machine, which comes pre-assembled and will create plastic products, spraying layers with powders similar to the technique used in ink jet printers. No shop floor; no shop employees.

This approach is being used for everything from office chairs in Norway to medical equipment. I recently saw an entire motorcycle that was 3D printed: I don't know how it would've stood up against a Harley long term, but it certainly suggests possibilities. UCLA is working on a project where the same approach will be used to build houses.

The progression continues, from huge River Rouge mass production plants employing thousands to job shops in the Pearl River Delta to, in a few years, a printer sitting on your desk (or in an Office Depot or FedEx, for larger objects) – ephemeralization is moving production from a building to a portion of your home office. We have met the future, and it needs a lot less real estate (to say nothing of a lot less hardware and workers).

Ephemeralization requires us all to add value, not just *process*. Seth Godin observed that *"it's essentially impossible to become successful or well-off doing a job that is described or measured by someone else."* This applies to companies as well as employees.

We're moving from the last vestiges of the Industrial Era to the Design Economy: value will be generated from concept and the rental of printing equipment, without physical assets or even staff. We're reaching the ultimate need for smart management and the ultimate non-competitiveness of mass production and low cost labor. This is potentially the biggest socio-economic shift since the Industrial Revolution, and I don't know one business that's fully prepared for it.

The financial area where ephemeralization applies is operating margin: the company that uses less financial assets to generate a given amount of profit (in other words, the company with the highest operating margin) is the company that will prove most successful and which will drive its less efficient competitors out of business. Assets and expenses only provide value when they help you produce cash flow streams.

You'll note that this is driven by financial productivity, not leverage. As we've seen recently, leverage works great until there's a problem – and then it doesn't work at all. The financial approaches that will succeed in global competition are the ones that can survive capital markets problems and market fluctuations. They are the ones that are most fiscally efficient.

IEDS AND OTHER EXPLOSIVE (BUSINESS) DEVICES

With most management problems, there's nothing that can't be solved by complete destruction of the existing order and radical re-assembly into a whole new approach. However, many management problems can't be solved by anything less. Inertia and failure of imagination have killed more companies than the Tech Bubble, Peak Oil and Jimmy Carter's creeping national malaise combined. In global competition, meek and unassuming solutions aren't going to feed the proverbial bulldog.

So let's get craaazy, shall we? With hard-core problems, we don't need rule books or a few training sessions. We need EXPLOSIVES. We need radical, absurd, insane change – which beats the Cheez Whiz™ out of unradical and polite collapse into obsolescence and liquidation.

There's a solution when it comes to business explosives. You've probably heard of IEDs (improvised explosive devices) in warfare, those nasty little gadgets that are regularly blowing up the Mideast. This book lays out IEDs for corporate problems, and (unlike both conventional IEDs and most management approaches) ours reduce casualties and costs instead of increasing them:

- Information: The more we know, the more effectively we can employ assets and the more we can avoid obvious mistakes. You won't trust all of the data you assemble, but you'll use it to generate initial moves and hypotheses you can test further. (We've had several clients accuse us of using great ingenuity to assemble math-based analyses which we then stubbornly refused to believe, and they're right – Popper's Falsity Principle remains alive and well.)

- Execution: All operating methods are not created equal – and they certainly don't all produce equal results. The more we use tested and effective approaches such as Lean and Agility, the more we'll increase throughput and reduce product variation. The result? Higher quality products produced for less cost.

- <u>Decisions</u>: Here's the tough one. In the trenches of global competition, we're faced with a million quick decisions in chaotic environments. How do we make the right ones? How do we make sure that our line employees are making the right decisions when we're not around, or that our global supply chain vendors are making the right decisions when they're twelve thousand miles away?

Information, Execution, Decisions. IED. Manage these three, and you create value – for your shareholders, your customers, your employees and yourself.

VI
INFORMATION
AND VALUE

Looking for villains preventing value creation is simple, but not very productive. Finger pointing is NOT the answer here. Most accountants and regulators and managers and workers want to do a good job; the failures we've seen don't result from greed or incompetence or any of the usual subjects. So why do so many problems end up with a batch of gesturing digits?

The issue here is a failure of systems. Many companies have information, but they can't use it. This occurs in several areas:

- The concept of financial information as a "snapshot of financial value": We manage better with stories than with portraits. Static data (a.) creates the illusion that the underlying reality is static as well, and (b.) misses the trends emerging from sequential data. Financial statements show a frozen moment, not actions. It would be hard to follow the plot twists of a movie that we only saw frame-by-frame, and it's hard to see the full implications of "frame by frame" operating data.

- Confusing models with reality: Korzybski noted that "the map is not the territory," and was then ignored by all the bankers and derivatives traders using formulas built on fixed relationships (which don't stay constant in shifting markets) and assumptions of efficient markets (which only occur on university blackboards). Executives who confuse maps (or models) with territory (or markets) better hit MapQuest looking for directions to a new career.

- Information versus Data: Information is focused. Information is actionable. Data is none of the above, consisting of huge piles of specific items that accumulate throughout most businesses. Modern executives are buried in data, but have no context or prioritization tools to extract information from the pile of unimportant specifics.

- Connection: When you see fixed data points, it's difficult to understand how they relate to other elements of the business. A carving knife slicing a carrot has less significance than the same knife held to your throat. Specifics matter.

Most systems obscure information instead of helping people use it. We need to consider better ways of working with operating statistics.

Fortunately, solutions for these issues became much more practical during the past decade. Low cost computing gives us tools that can do a lot of the crunching that once required account analysis and hand-crafting. Low cost/high capacity data storage allows us to work with large sets of detailed data in ways that would've been impossible a few years ago. And the expanded capacity of analytic tools ranging from Excel 2007 to Oracle Reports, Hyperion and the BW analytic package in SAP gives us means to take management and information usage to new levels of productivity. We still can't TRUST this stuff, but it gives us a starting point for management.

Let's consider these issues in the context of the first of our IED categories: information.

INFORMATION STARTS WITH DEFINITION

A pile of old shoes, a discarded Christmas tree, wadded newspapers, leaves, a spare tire, gravel, broken furniture, ripped clothes, tree stumps ... An assemblage of objects doesn't tell us much. Is it a garbage dump, or is it something useful?

To use something, we have to know what it is. We need to establish the limits of the possible: Will it fit? Is it metric or English? Decimal, binary, or octal? Can the floor take the weight? Will it match the color scheme? We move from garbage toward information when we start defining crisp measurements, operating instructions, or parameters. These tell us about limits.

To make any of this work in a business environment, we need to set limits:

a. Having clear measurements of our object's limits, and

b. Having a clear description of all the requirements our project needs to fill

You'll note that word, "clear". This element frequently gets overlooked in business crises. Descriptions such as "that's terrible!," "He's a good guy!," "I don't like it ... ," that Internet Era favorite "You don't get it ... ," or "That's rad, dude!" get substituted for usable limits.

This results in the much-feared management condition we addressed earlier known as MBA: Management By Adjectives. Descriptions of emotions, states and reactions take the place of useful characteristics, limits, and connections.Numbers and specifications become less attractive than impressions, vague and aspirational mission statements, and reactions.

MBA is apparently deeply attractive and fulfilling for many people, since we encounter it A LOT. They resent efforts to define issues and specifics, and (in our experience) feel personally wounded when someone wants to manage from definitions, numbers and specifics. This can be an issue in building corporate value, as we'll see later on.

VERIFYING INFORMATION

Yeah, "trust, but verify" once again. The greatest information system won't be so great if it contains complete rubbish. Making sure that your data elements are trustworthy involves a few standard issues.

Identify Bad Input: Garbage in; no usable information out. Bad input is anything that's inconsistent with other data you've already verified. It's incomplete (i.e., it doesn't give the whole "who, what, where, why, when, and how" that make it understandable and actionable). It's not timely: great data from the Eighteenth Century isn't applicable to current market issues.

(Note: If it's inconsistent *but can be verified*, this is a whole other issue. The weird but real items identify inflection points, new knowledge and lots of other important stuff ...)

Bad input is a given unless you define your metrics beforehand. Allowing users to decide what they've accomplished by selecting from un-designated elements after the fact (a.k.a., the way politicians analyze "results") doesn't allow users to improve decisions – you're navigating by guesses and assumptions.

Cross-check: Normalizing data (i.e., linking common data elements in one set to common elements in other sets that you've already collected) is common in database management. This is essential for addressing coding problems, ersatz entries, etc.

Sample: Data shouldn't be trusted simply because it's sitting in your system. There should be a periodic verification process pulling a sample of entries and going back to verify that they are actually correct.(I've learned this the hard way…)

INFORMATION THEORY

The application of these new tools – and the whole process of converting data to information – is driven by an analytic discipline called Information Theory, which was originally developed to increase the efficiency of telephone networks. It's useful in areas far beyond communications.

A core element of information theory is the relationship of "noise" (random, chaotic and unpredictable elements in a data set) to "signal" (the patterned, productive elements that we can use to accomplish goals). The higher the ratio of signal relative to noise, the more useful our system is.

Communications networks apply various processes ("filters") to extract the useful signal from the obscuring noise. As we'll see, similar approaches can be applied to the use of information in business.

Filtering applies to usage as well as the tools themselves. Users have structural limits imposed by the human brain that make filtering, focusing, and prioritization a necessity: our brains can't pay attention to more than a few factors at a given time, and there are definite boundaries on our ability to understand and make decisions from large numbers of discrete data elements. Fortunately, we don't have to. Data processing tools can help us cut through the clutter to the useful.

STRUCTURED INFORMATION

We get from "data" to "information" by filtering, by removing all the noise that isn't actionable, context-establishing, correct, or of any use. In most corporate data sites, this takes a lot of filtering.

Giant piles of corporate data specifics are dumped into "silos" that are arranged to look at those elements in fixed ways: accounting packages, customer relationship management ("CRM") systems, fixed asset packages, plus scores of largely-unmapped and poorly-coordinated Excel spreadsheets. This is (to be kind) a recipe for executive myopia.

Filtering this stuff starts with large chunks of that set theory stuff that confused the Hell out of schoolkids during the New Math era. Any schoolkids wanting to work with information need to get over that admittedly traumatic introduction, since databases and database queries are built on set theory concepts.

Most databases are operated and queried using something called "Structured Query Language," or SQL. A deep look at SQL is beyond the scope of our task here, but a basic glimpse at the way SQL puts together data searches tells us a lot about what we need to do in order to make our giant pile of data into something useful.

A SQL data extraction (or query) is built from three simple elements:

SELECT + FROM + WHERE

1. A SELECT component (which tells the system what sort of item you're looking for – a price, an inventory count for a particular SKU, a date or whatever). There can be more than one component built into a single SELECT statement.

2. A FROM component (which tells the system where to look for the items listed in the SELECT component), and

3. A WHERE component (which allows you to specify characteristics of the SELECT items that you want, allowing you to focus the search more closely than simply taking every file that falls in a SELECT category).

Okay, that's enough programming. And that's all we need – you can describe any search, including very complicated and specific ones, using permutations of these three components. This allows us to identify sets of items that have common elements.

How does this work for us in effectively operating a business?

In helping clients build greater corporate efficiency, we've found that a concept we call "structured information" solves many of these problems and produces consistently better operating results. The concept behind structured information is simple: store your data in a way that it can be accessed and sorted by non-technical users (i.e., the line workers who are making most of the specific decisions and doing most of the work in your organization).

Structured information can take place in a number of environments: databases, spreadsheets, abacuses (abacusi?), Web sites, Babbage Engines ... You name it. You've got structured information when the data elements meet some tests:

DATA IS ACCUMULATED AT THE SINGLE TRANSACTION LEVEL	There's a common tendency in business systems to work with summarized data elements: fields that are themselves summaries of other sets stored somewhere else entirely. This is a problem; unless you can link all the related issue to a lowest common denominator -- a sales invoice line, a patient encounter, a process step, a unit, or whatever -- you can't drill into the data or cross-sort with much power.
ALL DATA ELEMENTS ARE LINKED	General ledger entries are linked to sales detail are linked to shipping records are linked to warehouse data are linked to customer specifics are linked to commission payments. The more granular your raw entries, the easier this is (see above). Some elements aren't related directly to other, and allocations or interpolations will be required. The initial setup takes work, but can be mantained by clerical manpower once it's established.
THE SYSTEM NEEDS TO PROVIDE A COMPONENT TRAIL	Users generally deal with higher categories: P & L statements by SKU or customer, or buyer characteristics for a set of SKUs, or whatever. To under-stand what they're seeing, they need the cabability to "drill down" into the high level figures to see the entries that compose them. This is why we need all that granularity referred to above. Larger accounting systems such as SAP are built around drill down features. Smaller companies can achieve drill down with relative ease using pivot tables in Excel 2007.
THE SYSTEM NEEDS TO BE CONTEXT-DRIVEN	Layout of the system needs to vary depending on how the user is applying it. Linking data to browser-based user interfaces is a simple way of achieving this; its also possible with reporting packages (for higher end packages) or Excel (in smaller company environments).
THE SYSTEM NEEDS TO BE USER DRIVEN	The key issue here is that AN IT MANAGER OR CFO IS NOT A USER. When a system doesn't give users what they want, they won't use the system. Acting as a censor for the less-educated is tempting, but destructive to the workforce skill base, to communications, and to the company's ability to perform.

If your data elements meet these conditions, you can determine how they're related to each other. This allows you to understand when they're useful, when they're relevant, and how they connect to specific business conditions and operations.

STRUCTURED INFORMATION ENVIRONMENTS

The most common environment for structured data is in the reporting engine of the financial system. This isn't necessarily the BEST environment: non-financial factors such as Operational or Marketing data may be critical to decision-making. So you'll have to integrate financial data with various other operating statistics. There are several common structures for accumulating this data in a common source:

1. Data Warehouse: This can be any collection of databases, linked databases, accounting and CRM systems, or other digital sources that contain relevant data and are regularly updated. We've seen some clients do this through a "reporting database" that also served as backup to the primary information environments (automatically pulling the required data from the primary sources nightly so users would have data that's not more than 24 hours old). One of the advantages of this "mirror warehouse" approach is it ensures that unsophisticated users get the information they need without being in a position where they can damage primary data.

2. Data Mart: This can either be a separate database or a partitioned repository within the main database. Again, the theory is that you ensure user functionality without endangering the primary source input.

3. Metadata Repository: This contains technical information and a data definition (i.e., source, unit of measurement, etc.) This (a.) is a tool to make sure that all of the sources are normalized and talking about the same things in the same way, and (b.) is a primary resource in sampling initiatives and other data quality/data verification efforts.

None of these is the best solution for all possible situations. Which one you'll use depends on the specifics of your environment (including what reporting systems you've already got in place).

CREATING STRUCTURED INFORMATION

Structure requires work. Even a simple structured information process requires a number of steps that don't take place in conventional accounting, shipping, or shop floor operations. Having said that, they don't take a lot of additional time; we've created structured information systems in $500 million companies that were maintained by an additional 30 to 40 man-hours per month.

The cost? Thirty to 40 hours of accounting clerk. The avoidance of bad decisions and the quick access to key information needed to resolve crises? Worth A LOT. (Note: The 40 hours per month spent organizing the data was more than recovered through avoidance of various business planning people burning hours to build custom reports in answer to user queries that can be generated within seconds through a few clicks in a structured data environment ...)

The additional steps look something like the following, depending on the specifics of company operations:

- Normalize all of your data between sources (i.e., determining common data elements in general ledger detail, sales invoice records, commission records, shipping records, fixed asset management systems, etc.) which can be used to join elements in different sources.

- Link all of the data sources by common elements so

the entire data set can be searched and analyzed by user-set guidelines. This approach is built to allow "drill down" capabilities such as the ones featured in SAP, so high level numbers can be broken down into their components to ensure users know what specifics are in the summary information. (Note: This isn't particularly difficult: pivot tables in Excel can be easily set to provide full "drill down" functionality. OLAP cubes can also be configured to provide this in a number of database environments.)

- Have multiple data sets for different time periods available, so that patterns can be extracted. The current data sets should be as dynamic as possible; minimizing the "lag" between the current period (when people are making decisions) and the data period (when the last data was accumulated).

- Set up the final data environment so that it's accessible by general users throughout the company – no IT or Finance specialists being required for a company line staff member to access information regarding a problem affecting their job. (Note: This DOES require that the data environment allow different authorization levels, so that people aren't accessing confidential information that isn't directly related to their job ...)

- Users are supported with guidance, not censorship. This is a shift for many Accounting departments dominated by the Controller mindset (i.e., we must keep the unwashed line workers under strict control by limiting information access). There is a cost to organizational stupidity which regularly outstrips the cost of people working with raw data. The best way to minimize problems from poor use of information is to assign Business Planning analysts to do their core job: help people resolve problems with financial information, and make sure they understand the numbers when they try to use them. The more this process takes place, the more intelligent the decisions will be at the line level and the fewer problems due to confusion, misunderstanding, or poor skills in information interpreting and analysis.

The result allows users to understand why their information looks as it does, and what is contained in specific items. This helps them make better decisions, avoid misunderstandings and mistakes, and builds better analytic and planning capabilities throughout the company.

Structured information takes a bit more work from Finance and IT (though it also saves a lot of work from account analysis and special report creation ...)   The extra effort provides substantial corporate dividends. Data analysts evaluating computer networks make use of a concept called Metcalfe's Law, which states:

"The value of the network is proportional to the square of the number of nodes."

What this means is that, when information items are linked together, their utility/value to users grows at a logarithmic rate/"hockey stick curve"/high compounding factor. A little extra effort produces a lot more value. This applies to business processes as well as business networks.

FOCUS: KEY FACTORS IN EVALUATING BUSINESS PERFORMANCE

Users can seldom apply every available fact about a given business element; it's often useful to pare down their first look at information to factors that are most likely to affect business performance. (As noted above, drill-down features keep this approach from masking important details.)

In general, the factors most related to corporate performance are found in four areas:

1. Value: This includes both the tangible value (physical assets and cash flow streams) and intangible value (intellectual property, relationships, rights, etc.) of a business component. In theory, these components should underlie the fair value of the component.

2. Context: Also known as "scope," this includes the potential areas where future value can be extracted (or lost) from changes in management of the component.

3. Volatility: These are the operating risk elements: How stable are the value and context of the component? How accurately are they understood, and how radically could they change?

4. Timing: Time is money. Modern executives – and modern business initiatives – don't have forever to execute. Evaluation of business options includes assessment of how quickly they can be completed and whether they're on track for completion.

While these categories don't address all possible issues, they cover many of the critical ones. If management processes are structured to always address these considerations, the business can move quickly to manage opportunities and problems.

HOW DOES THIS WORK IN A BUSINESS ENVIRONMENT?

Knowledge is power. This is often a factor in corporate political struggles; one executive will often attempt to grab control of all contact with data, and dole out data elements to suit their agenda. This is a workable tactic but a lousy strategy: the executive in question gains power while destroying the functionality of the company that's his power base.

There's a lesser-known corollary to this well-known statement – that ignorance is power transferred to all the companies competing with yours. Keeping your co-workers uninformed (and therefore making uninformed decisions) isn't a basis for corporate or personal greatness. Business power is driven by solid understanding of the working parts of the organization and their impact on business value – in every part of the organization.

The playoff between these two factors will drive the success of a structured data initiative. Life is usually much easier if you plan this through before the initiative starts.

STRUCTURED INFORMATION: NOPAT, EVA AND BEYOND

Financial performance is Ground Zero: the most critical of all business information in need of structure and context. Happy employees and positive customer perception are important, but unless an executive produces yield for the shareholders they take the toys away – which means that all of the rest is interesting but not quite as important.

Financial performance ... We've already noted that GAAP doesn't provide sufficient information. What does? A common answer in recent years has been "Economic Value Added," or "EVA," the analysis method popularized by the Sloan Stewart consulting firm and defined as "net operating profit after taxes less the cost of capital."

This approach addresses many of my objections to GAAP. It knocks out many of the weirder GAAP conventions (since net operating profit is derived only from the firm's operations, and doesn't include investment income or loss, though practitioners differ on whether it should include items such as capitalized brand advertising.) It focuses on investment yield and it considers the opportunity cost of capital by capital class (i.e., by debt, stock, or whatever). This is positive stuff, and is a good start to providing management with necessary information. But it's only a start.

The most common objection to EVA is that it can be distorted by poor risk evaluation. A shift to equity capital from debt will often decrease the value of the company under EVA, even though there's a default risk in debt that isn't in equity and may not be correctly priced. I'd also note two other issues:

1. EVA views the company from a very high level: it's driven by NOPAT, which doesn't include the operational detail driving the final number. This leaves management is seeing THAT a change took place without having a clue as to WHY it happened.

2. EVA still works from a "snapshot of value" perspective which is more useful to a lender than an operator. It doesn't identify trends or correlations.

DYNAMIC COSTING

What's an alternative? My consulting firm's had success using something called Dynamic Costing. The idea with Dynamic Costing is simple: create a structured information system where you can analyze the business value of each business component (i.e., each customer, each product, or whatever). This allows you to understand what specific elements of your business are profitable or losing money. More importantly, it lets your employees understand the same thing so they won't destroy business value through ignorance.

There are some problems in doing this, and many of them result from an area we've already noted: accounting principles.

ABSORPTION COST METHODS
AND OPERATIONS MANAGEMENT

When our hearts were young, the world was green, and the FASB was deciding how to handle inventory issues, it decreed that something called "full absorption accounting" should be barred by GAAP from use as a reporting technique. ("Full absorption accounting," to oversimplify a bit, is an approach allocating costs to revenues in inventory issues).

FASB's concern was understandable – they didn't want to allow financial engineering of inventory numbers to allow unscrupulous managers (which, in the post-Enron era, apparently means damn near everybody in management) to manipulate earnings.

However, the method they used to do it also barred GAAP statements from creating direct coupling of all operating costs to profits, which is needed to create financial statements for specific functions or products. Sales costs, for example, can't be directly linked *as a cost* to the revenue from the sale. This makes it difficult to create statements that provide much clarity into operating effectiveness. That's not a problem for your banker, but it leaves your executive team working with some seriously opaque data.

This is a fundamental issue. If (a.) GAAP is intentionally disconnected from management accounting, and (b.) most companies spend so much time on financier-required GAAP reporting that they never get to management accounting, we've got a lot of companies operating on guesses rather than knowledge when they figure where they make or lose money. Not good.

So conventional financial statements only show the financial condition of the entire company. Maybe they break out some key divisions if they want to look detailed. They tell you HOW the entire company is doing, but they don't tell you WHY.

Effective managements aren't just evaluating creditworthiness. They're trying to build it. This takes another approach entirely. They need the data linking that's barred under full absorption accounting rules. Instead of credit-based financial statements, they need a set of Dynamic Costing statements that focus on where they are making and losing money:

A financial statement for each SKU
A financial statement for each customer
A financial statement for each piece of equipment
A financial statement for each salesperson
A financial statement for each patent or copyright
A financial statement for each zip code

They can combine these elements (i.e., a financial statement for specific SKUs sold through a certain channel). More importantly, they can be re-configured dynamically to drill into unexpected results and relationships.

Suddenly, people have the information to maximize profits, lower their operating risk exposure, and generally bring forth the Millennium. They can see what's working, and what isn't.

Dynamic Costing is the financial version of a software concept called object oriented programming, which is used in efficiently writing computer code. Object oriented programming allows individual lines of code to be re-used in different ways to solve problems as they occur. In Dynamic Costing, the components – the transactions, in the case of financial records – are created in a similar way allowing them to be combined and re-used to get the desired results.

About now, the accounting types in the audience are thinking that this sounds a lot like activity-based costing ("ABC") – and they're right. A lot of similar ideas. But the differences between Dynamic Costing and activity-based costing tell us a lot about tool use and results-based management.

WHY DID ACTIVITY-BASED COSTING FAIL?

ABC is one of those ideas that's been around forever but never really took off. Since the issues it addresses – figuring out where you made and lost money – are so basic, this seems surprising. Why doesn't everyone use ABC?

The answer becomes a little more apparent when we think about how classic ABC works. It's built around three primary concepts:

☐ <u>Cost Pool</u> = A group of ledger accounts that are related (they act in a similar manner and are often organized by department). Cost pools contain the resource inputs for the organization. An example would be hourly labor, salaried labor, vacation, and overtime all being grouped as "wages." These are usually overhead and SG&A expenses, and not direct materials or labor costs.

☐ Driver = A measure (tracked with numbers, not adjectives) that shows a process or activity which triggers use ("consumption") of a cost pool. (The number of sales or purchase orders or insurance claims could trigger process usage for manufacturing or insurance companies, for example). Drivers are the result of transactions or events, and they have a very close cause and effect relationship to (a.) a particular cost pool, and (b.) a cost object. They become the logical link between the two. Drivers differ from "allocation" (the traditional way to spread expenses in GAAP accounting) because they're specific: they're generated by defined and quantifiable business activities rather than general and arbitrary formulae.

☐ Cost Object = An attribute of a transaction we're trying to value. This could be a product, a vendor, a facility, a customer channel, a region or other component. Cost Objects consume activities like the consumption of Cost Pools by Drivers.

These concepts are then linked to develop the activity-based statements. This looks complicated, but is simply:

a. Taking related costs
b. Identifying the factors that cause them, and
c. Relating them to the revenues or cash yields of the business

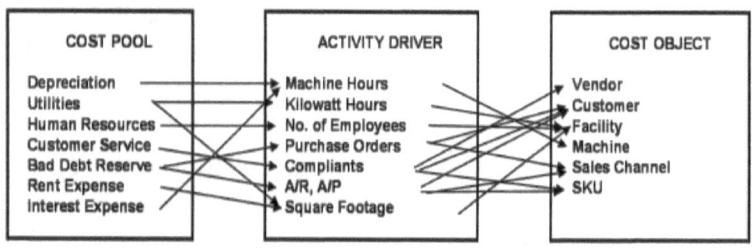

This gets you important information, but DOESN'T make an easy life for whoever pulls the short straw and has to assemble the activity driver data. This stuff isn't tracked in most companies, and requires either (a.) detailed input from line employees who will distrust and resist the entire process, or (b.) use of electronic alternatives (RFID or bar coding, coupled with cost-intensive modifications of whatever ERP system's in use) which involve substantial up front expenses and process disruption.

There is also a second set of problems, and this relates to upper management. Any scorekeeping process produces winners and losers. Any NEW scorekeeping process produces DIFFERENT winners and losers than you've got right now.

Some managers don't want more accountability: division heads, department leaders, sales heads, operating guys ... You name it. Some people get nervous when it's too easy to look over their shoulders, and they'll do what they can to make shoulder surfing as difficult as possible. They'll create obstacles for the process.

WHY WILL DYNAMIC COSTING WORK WHERE ABC WON'T?

The answer to this issue is surprisingly simple: Dynamic Costing avoids detailed information requirements for accumulating activity driver data.

The Rule of All Rules for executives is that old favorite: the 80-20 Rule. Eighty percent of all the good stuff comes from 20% of the work. A few key points produce most of the results. When you build that into the process, life gets much more practical.

You work with close approximations. You take input from managers regarding ratios of work, of unit flow, and build those ratios into the calculation. You're sensible and close to reality, but fixed costs aren't related *"exactly"* to specific acts the way they would be if you actually developed the RFID and ERP ("Enterprise Resource Planning") capabilities to track absolutely every action in the company. The result won't be perfection, but it will show you those 80% of the problems where you're losing money on products, assets, customers or people. And you'll get the information FAST, when you need it.

Pardon me. That commotion you just heard in the background was the armed rebellion of classical accounting types screaming "That's not PRECISE!!!" and waving general ledger printouts in a threatening and intimidating manner. Dear, dear. They apparently forgot that accruals also aren't precise, nor are tax carryforward assets (which are, after all, contingent on future events), charges for options or any number of things that are standard operating procedure with GAAP.

Imprecision's part of the game. Once you get comfortable with that, you can use "pretty good" numbers to make a lot better decisions than you could if you attempted to achieve some Platonic ideal of Absolute Financial Truth. If your model can be "tuned" and adjusted when you get further data, it will get even better.

You can also avoid some big problems, and find where you're making money which you didn't expect. An example is a project managed by Gregg Martins, one of my consulting firm's partners. Gregg's client was a little manufacturing company that had two operating divisions: auto aftermarket and aerospace. Management was sure that aerospace was where the profits were, and started setting up the auto aftermarket division for sale.

Gregg's assignment was to build the costing analysis to show exactly where the aerospace operation was most profitable (though he was also analyzing the auto aftermarket operation while he was at it). They agreed to simplified allocations, and (as a result) the project got completed within 45 days. The results were very useful to company management, though not in the way they expected:

a.   The auto aftermarket products had some strong, profitable lines of business, and

b.   There wasn't anything in aerospace that was even covering its variable costs. Every dollar of aerospace business they booked was eroding net worth – and sale of the auto aftermarket division would've killed the company.

If the company had waited until they got the resources to create a full activity-based costing analysis, the auto aftermarket division would've been sold and they would've been dead before they knew it. Because they followed the 80 – 20 Rule, they saved themselves from a company-killing mistake.

WHAT'S THE RESULT?

The result of a Dynamic Costing program is a system that will produce financial statements by any set of breakouts that can be derived from the underlying interlinked data:

Example Categories

Channel	(All)
Customer_Type	(All)
Customer_Posting_Group	(All)
Product_Group_Code	(All)
Sell_to_Customer_Name	(All)
Sales_Rep	(All)
Gen_Prod_Posting_Group	(All)
Product_Type	(All)
Requisition_Method_Code	(All)
Product_Class_Code	(All)
Product_Status	(All)
Vendor_Retail_Packaged	(All)
Phone_ID_Make	(All)
Phone_ID_Model	(All)
Manufacturer_Code	(All)
No_	(All)
Description	(All)
Inventory_Status	(All)
Vendor_Posting_Group	(All)
Vendor_Name	(All)
Purchaser_Code	(All)
Responsibility_Center	(All)

The final statements are generated by selection of the relevant category.

In full ERP systems, this is done in reporting modules such as BW or Business Objects or in specialty add-ons like OROS, COGNOS, Business Objects or Hyperion. But this can also be done in Excel 2007 using pivot tables, which can be set and operated by non-skilled users to create whichever statements are desired. The new Excel has considerably larger capacity than earlier versions – 1 million lines and 15,000 columns (though all of this isn't accessible to pivot tables) – and is large enough that we've created detailed dynamic costing analyses for companies with $400 million in annual revenues and 30,000 SKUs using Excel.

In deciding what environment you're going to use, you need to think through the trade-offs between on-line analytical processing ("OLAP") in large systems and pivot tables in spreadsheets. This isn't a simple trade-off determination; there are strengths to both environments:

OLAP	PIVOT TABLES
Fully scalable (no upper limit to capacity)	Limited to 500,000 lines of data and 1,048,576 items
High initial cost of system and implementation/roll out	Standard part of Microsoft Office
Database components can be set up in open source (though this requires more SQL programming talent)	Limited to ODBC-compliant sources though this includes many standard databases
Smaller base of trained operators; more expensive staff are required and will take more time to recruit	Large user base familiar with the format
Easily linked to other SQL-compliant systems	Adaptable to ODBC-linkable databases
Requires larger-format IT environments	Can be driven in smaller departments with non-technical staffing
"Set it and forget it" configuration	Easily adaptable/re-configurable

Regardless of the environment used, the end result is a financial statement by operating object that can be operated by non-technical users, allowing them to generate a wide variety of customized reports after a few minutes of training:

Data	Total
Quantity	3,230,842
ASP	$7.55
GROSS INVOICES	$ 24,732,857
GROSS CREDIT MEMOS	$ (354,355)
GROSS SALES	$ 24,378,502
Credit Memo Pct%	-1.4%
PRICE ADJ./DISCOUNTS	$ (25,674)
RETURNS & ALLOWANCES	$ (759,759)
CUSTOMER INCENTIVES	$ (1,117,351)
REV SHARE	$ (205,160)
Sales Discounts/Allowances/Incentives Total	$ (2,107,943)
Sales Adjustments Other Pct%	-8.6%
NET SALES	$ 22,270,559
GROSS COGS	$ 18,572,846
COGS ADJ/DEF/BAL	$ (697,338)
COGS E & O	$ (50,000)
COGS PKG/SAMPLES	$ 96,683
COGS REBATES/PP	$ (577,546)
BIZDEV - BEST BUY REBATE	$ (30,000)
COGS RECON	$ 26,005
COGS Returns/Adj/Rebates & Other Total	$ (1,232,196)
COGS Adjustments Other Pct%	-5.1%
NET COGS	$ 17,340,650
GROSS MARGIN	$4,929,909
ACP	$5.37
GM Percent	20.2%
GM PER UNIT	$ 1.53
FREIGHT - OUT	$ 474,478
FREIGHT - IN	$ 519,852
TEMP LABOR	$ 332,454
SALES COMMISSIONS	$ 96,522
Other Variable Costs	$ 1,423,306
Variable Cost Pct%	5.8%
CONTRIBUTION MARGIN	$3,506,603
CM Percent	14.4%
PR-SHP	$ 47,514
PR-ASS	$ 215,774
PR-WAR	$ 126,911
PR-REC	$ 19,806
PR-QAS	$ 46,546
PR-ADM	$ 116,378
TOTAL PLANT EXPENSES	$ 572,929
PLANT EXPENSE PERCENT	2.4%
SL-OUT	$ 81,348
SL-INS	$ 90,285
SL-SUP	$ 88,877
SL-REP	$ 553
SL-ADM	$ 135,098
CUSSVC	$ 93,604
PMGMKT	$ 173,127
MRKTNG	$ 254,394
BIZDEV	$ 74,585
TOTAL SELLING EXPENSES	$ 991,871
SELLING EXPENSE PERCENT	4.1%
PURCHS	$ 116,920
CHN-SZ	$ 115
ENGRNG	$ 200,424
RESDEV	$ 65,385
SUPCHN	$ 112,597
TOTAL PRODUCT EXPENSES	$ 495,441
PRODUCT EXPENSE PERCENT	2.0%
INTECH	$ 158,516
FINANC	$ 274,144
ADMINI	$ 119,855
TOTAL G&A EXPENSES	$ 552,515
G&A EXPENSE PERCENT	2.3%
EBITA	$ 893,846
INTEREST EXPENSE	$ 74,196
INCOME TAXES	$ 29,417
DEPR./AMORT.	$ 68,990
NET INCOME	$721,244
NET INCOME PERCENT	3.0%
NET INCOME PER UNIT	$0.22

This example was generated by a user wanting high granularity; you can narrow down the number of categories if your people want to work with a less detailed summary. The statement should include what's most useful for your department heads in making their decisions.

Where does this get you? The larger scale result is that management understands the connection between one of its basic goals (maximizing the excess of revenues over costs) and business operations. Activities are linked to financial results.

This approach isn't limited to financial issues. Linking of specific marketing programs to subsequent sales (or to subsequent PROFITABLE sales); linking of increases in returns or scrap rates to specific actions ... Once your information is:

- Connected

- Fully searchable

- Spanning an extended period of time

you can use it to make better decisions by linking actions and outcomes. It won't give you certainty, but it will increase your understanding.

FIXED VS. VARIABLE

A key element in these statements is the breakout of variable costs (those directly related to the creation of a specific product or service) and fixed costs (those general costs of running a business that go on whether anything is produced or not).

A simple example of a fixed versus variable cost breakdown looks something like this:

```
┌──────────────────────────────────────────────────┐
│                                                    │
│    TOTAL CORPORATE COSTS                           │
│                                                    │
│                                                    │
│ VARIABLE                                           │
│     Materials                                      │
│     Manufacturing Labor                            │
│     Scrap                                          │
│     Outside Prossessing & Supplies                 │
│     Equipment Maintenance & Depreciation           │
│     Quality Control                                │
│                                                    │
│                                                    │
│ FIXED                                              │
│     Sales                                          │
│     Accounting & Finance                           │
│     Executive                                      │
│     Facilities Costs                               │
│                                                    │
└──────────────────────────────────────────────────┘
```

There's obviously some room for category variations in this approach (where do you put financing costs for the equipment? Where do you put something like warranty expense?), but these can be defined and documented as a "standard" for your company. The algorithm will then be written to distribute in accordance with that "standard," and Dynamic Costing statements splitting the variable and fixed costs can be created.

Why is this important? The main issue is Contribution to Surplus: the concept that a product can be unprofitable (i.e., its revenues don't support the combination of variable costs and all of the allocated fixed costs), but still bring in more than its variable costs which means that it is paying at least part of the fixed expenses. This is useful when making "kill it or keep it" decisions.

When you see Contribution to Surplus issues, this tells you to be on the lookout for certain classes of problems:

1. Your allocation method for fixed costs may be questionable (i.e., if you have products that are unprofitable only because of fixed cost allocation, while the overall company is profitable).

2. Some products are creating a lot of administrative overhead, or

3. Your overhead costs aren't supportable, in which case you need to figure out how to lower them.

Management uses financial statements to manage. The more quickly and effectively the statements aim managers at specific operations problems, the more useful they are in running the company day-to-day. This gets overlooked when everyone's thinking about statements as a part of the financing – but the company needs to apply proceeds after they're raised, and use them to generate enough share value to offset the cost of capital. You won't do that with a standard statement. You CAN use structured information to accomplish this.

RETURN ON INVESTMENT AND HURDLE RATES

As we noted, it's critical to understand where you're making or losing money. This is what Dynamic Costing tells you. But it's important to place those figures in context.

The basic measure for this is return on investment, just as we all learned in those first finance courses. This is where we get back to the issues raised by EVA. The key here is to drive the analysis by operating object – by the business components and operations that make or lose money – rather than looking at the overall company.

Components you can manage; the overall business you can only buy, sell or close – which isn't useful for most executives.

Operating objects need to offer a better risk-adjusted return on investment than any reasonable alternative. This is the idea behind hurdle rates, the concept that earnings need to achieve a specified level or the money can be put to better uses elsewhere. It extends the ideas behind EVA into an operating context. This is a useful concept for executives, and is even more useful for shareholders.

IS THIS JUST ABOUT FINANCE?

I've addressed the financial side of structured data because it's critical for executives. But this doesn't mean that structured information is purely a financial tool.

Modern plant operations are driven by information. Operations tools such as Lean (Toyota Manufacturing System) and Agile techniques are heavily driven by numerical tracking of performance. Six Sigma is built around statistical analysis of execution. Supply Chain success is largely a function of maintaining and acting on information. In all of these areas, structured information techniques can make information easily to compile, locate and apply.

MARKETING DATA

In Marketing (as opposed to Sales, Advertising, Graphics, and the many other fields which people still confuse with actual Marketing), information analysis is critical. Effective Marketing programs are built on a foundation of solid customer understanding. This, in turn, is built on effective capture, manipulation, and analysis of information: determining what actually happens when people decide to buy (or not buy) the product through analysis of detailed sales and demographic data. Again, structured information techniques can deliver better decisions and fewer mistakes with less effort.

The basic questions driving Marketing success are the questions that basic journalism is supposed to answer: who, what, where, when and why. However, solving them in Marketing is much more difficult than delivering the news: "the news" can be descriptive without being specific or quantitative, but workable Marketing data needs to be precise and defined enough to be actionable (and accurate enough not to sink the company through mistakes).

Marketing data assembly is far more difficult than with Finance. Definitions in financial elements are fairly tightly defined (though, as we've seen when considering GAAP, "fairly" is a long way from "exactly").Definitions in Marketing are far more cloudy.

Data must also address two different issues: quantitative (the specifics of particular sales and promotional programs) and psychographic (the more mysterious aspects of why specific people made or rejected specific purchases).

For all of the neuro-marketing, focus groups and the rest, psychographic analysis in Marketing remains a Black Art mastered by the Elect, the Chosen, the Truly Stylish, or the Lucky Guessers. There are situations where application of Black Arts beats the Hell out of utter ignorance – but even here the conversation needs to be shaped by a combination of deep customer understanding (Black Art), deep understanding of the whole problem (design and engineering), plus – wait for it! – a bunch of relevant data from actual purchases in the real world.

Purchase data remain a deep disappointment to us all. There's lots of data being sold out there, and all of it is flawed:

The Regionality Problem: For some products, services such as Nielsen have better sampling in some parts of the country than others. Extending the findings from areas where you have samples to areas where you don't may be unavoidable, but involves risk.

The "True Customer" Problem: In industries ranging from software to liquor, the brand owner reaches the customer through a three-tier model (with a distributor, value-added reseller, or other middleman sitting between the actual purchaser and the company). In these cases, analyses of your internal sales detail (which is normally your most detailed source of data) won't drill down to the end purchaser (who you may never see). Technical products can get around this with warranty information, but retail products have to work carefully through the imperfections of their data sources.

The Definition Problem: Since Marketing doesn't have an equivalent of generally accepted accounting principles, information is aggregated by different folks using different approaches. As the end user, you need to make sure that you're not combining apples and applesauce when you're creating analyses from this stuff.

Integrating Research Data and Quantitative Data: News flash! People act differently when they're being questioned about sales preferences than when they actually buy stuff. You have role-playing and public persona issues and perceived peer pressure, as well as the definitional issues we noted above.Proceed with caution.

Resolving all of these issues in a single, short term project is unlikely, but every one that's addressed is one less opportunity for ignorance, misunderstanding, confusion, inflection point shifts or other unseen variables to damage the company.

When we break down our basic questions – who, what, where, when and why – and examine the detail implied and the issues which arise from that detail, it's evident that quantitative marketing analysis is an ongoing and evolving process.But these questions can be translated into quantitative items which can be used for better decision-making, as is shown in the following example:

CATEGORY	SPECIFICS	ISSUES
WHO	. Demographics . Sales by Demographic Element . Gross Margin by Demographic Element . Returns by Demographic Element . SKU by Demographic Element	. Accessing lists or databases
WHAT	. Sales by SKU . Gross Margin by SKU . Returns by SKU . Sales by Product Bundle . Gross Margin by Product Bundle . Returns by Product Bundle	. Unit of Measure . Close of Sale Timing . Shipped vs. Depletions
WHERE	. Sales by Channel . Gross Margin by Channel . Returns by Channel . Sales by Campaign . Gross Margin by Campaign . Returns by Campaign . Sales by Zip Code . Gross Margin by Zip Code . Returns by Zip Code . Sales by Channel Category . Gross Margin by Channel Category . Returns by Channel Category	. What other events were happening at the site of the sale? . What local/regional events affect perception and consumption patterns
WHY	. Common elements of effective campaigns . Common elements of effective channels . Common elements of failed campaigns . Common elements of failed channels . Correlation to other puchases	. Establishing single causative variables . Establishing causation from correlation

Your specific marketing situation may rely on different indicators. The key here is to think about the basic questions and develop crisp numerical measures that clarify them.

OPERATIONS INFORMATION

Shop floor execution is precise. The execution of processes can be accurately measured.The problems that arise are:

a.   You've got people who AREN'T precise. They don't do things consistently, and they don't track what they do.

b.   You've got supervisors who are more concerned with getting goods out the door (whether or not those goods meet specs) than knowing what happens in the area they're supervising. Garbage thinking in, garbage products out.

c.   You've got weird stuff that happens and isn't documented.

But understanding is driven by information on a production floor. The great productivity improvements of the past half century, from Deming and Juran forward, are driven by numbers. Manufacturing has a similar issue to every other part of the company: if you don't understand what happened (i.e., what produced the result, and the process that created the result), you'll do a mediocre job of managing anything. If you're using an outside vendor, they need the same customer feedback that you do.

Accumulating production floor information is becoming easier. While job tickets or "travelers" have a long history of being ignored or not filled in correctly (there's always a crisis that's more important than knowing what the Hell you're doing), bar codes and RFID are working in environments from warehouses to hospitals. The equipment for all of this is amazingly cheap – and the alternative (i.e., ignorance) is amazingly expensive.

INFORMATION HOARDING

This issue doesn't go away. We can use information to improve every department in a business – if we can get the information. But, as we've noted, many departmental or divisional leaders feel they must control the information in order to maintain power: access to information is controlled, data elements are defined, and usually presented in fixed formats that are difficult to quickly analyze.

This is inevitably deadly to corporate performance. Executives are betting their company when they allow this: lack of information must be investigated, solutions developed, information needs to be circulated to users throughout the company, and zero tolerance policies for data strangulation need to be adopted and enforced.

WHOSE INFORMATION IS IT, ANYWAY?

Information hoarding inside a company is a clear problem, but the issue becomes more complex for companies built on the "Hollywood Model": the team approach between groups of expert contractors or joint venturers who co-operate on particular products or markets, but maintain separate corporate entities.

There aren't any easy answers here. Open exchange of data becomes steadily more necessary as groups in different locations collaborate on short deadlines.

Companies such as shoe retailer Zappos see this as a big plus, noting "It's like having an extra 1,500 pairs of eyes to help us manage the business." The downside is that those 1,500 pairs of eyes get to see product failures, suppliers' environmental problems, labor disputes, consumer activist flame wars and all the other ugly impedimenta of modern corporate operations on a real time basis. That may be a good thing – nothing keeps peoples' eyes on customer responsiveness like the clear and certain knowledge that the whole world is watching – but corporations should think carefully about what they're letting themselves in for.

VII
EXECUTION:
DO IT YOURSELF

KNOW THYSELF

Management is, they tell us, is the art of getting other people to do what you want them to. The key word here is "do." The greatest of plans and the most worthy of intents mean little if you didn't accomplish your goals.

Getting from where you are (i.e., your present situation) to your goal (i.e., your heart's desire) requires that you (a.) know where you are now, (b.) know where you want to go, and (c.) you go there. This is more difficult than it sounds; many organizations have little idea of exactly where they want to go. They have adjectives; they have uplifting phrases and visions of share price. What they don't have is defined deliverables.

Most modern systems for process management focus on this issue at the start of the effort. A standard project approach works something like this:

1. IDENTIFY PRESENT STATE

- Map processes.
- Identify assets.
- Perform capability analysis (i.e., determine the limits of what can be performed right now with the current assets deployed in the current system).

2. IDENTIFY FUTURE STATE

- Define specifics (these not only include specific performance factors but can include lifestyle and other intangibles).
- Define critical elements required to achieve desired specifics.

3. IDENTIFY THE PROCESS PATH THAT GETS YOU FROM PRESENT STATE TO FUTURE STATE

That third factor's a little more complex than the first two. It's easy to recognize how screwed up things are now, and it's easier still to dream. It's harder to actualize.

THE EVOLVING ORGANIZATION

The classic approach for process planning is the one in the standard business plan: various standard categories are described, followed by a linear process outlining, one after the next, the steps that will take us to certain victory. Fans of the Domino Theory and the Vietnam War may recognize the layout. It's technically referred to as a "waterfall plan," with each step cascading down to the next until it reaches the end.

Like a waterfall, there's much about this process that's all wet. Its primary fault is that it requires perfect prediction of the future to work; each step depends on the successful execution of the one before. Psychohistory stirs its ugly head, and Clausewitz, "the fog of war" and "the first casualty of any conflict is the plan of battle" are raising their hands and waving.

A corollary to the waterfall project plan is the concept of "staying the course"; of believing that, with sufficient guts, determination, true grit, and monomaniacal focus on following the initially-determined path, even the most complex and unlikely of plans will eventually work. In politics, this approach brought us the Vietnam War and Iraq. In business, it drove the management of Detroit automakers, network television broadcasters, and other folks who believe that "If we build it they will come" was more than a cinematic trivia footnote.

So what replaces the Domino Theory?

The most successful approach is derived from a chunk of math called iterative transforms, which points out that you can get powerful and unexpected results from simply trying lots of different inputs to some basic equations. In the real world, this results in a process that Ross Perot used to refer to as:

READY – FIRE - AIM

This isn't intuitive, but it is effective. The process is just what it sounds like:

1.   Make preparations and get **ready** to try something

2.   **Fire** (i.e., actually try it), and

3.   See what actually happened and **aim** to adjust your approach to reality and improve it

The non-liberal arts majors in the crowd will recognize this as a permutation of the Scientific Method:

1. Create a hypothesis (i.e., **ready**)

2. Test the hypothesis (i.e., **fire**)

3. Analyze the results

4. Adjust your hypothesis to reflect your findings (i.e., **aim**)

They'll also recognize it as Evolutionary: an optimal plan developed through successive attempts and fine-tuned by learning and experience, rather than a plan created through a single perfect and infallible vision. The nice thing about evolution, transforms and the Scientific Method is that they WORK. They have a long history of producing results. Recent management tools incorporate the strength of these elements into their approach, and use them in producing new sets of results to add to the record.

CONTINUOUS QUALITY IMPROVEMENT

The emphasis on multiple editions and ongoing learning that we saw above is one of the keystones of current operations management: continuous quality improvement. I'm going to avoid the history; suffice it to say that a number of post-World War II manufacturing engineers, notably W. Edwards Deming and Joseph M. Juran, recognized that mass production and top-down management were dropping the ball on fabricating products without costly scrap and rework.While this seems a real yawner at this point, it was truly startling when originated, which is why U.S. business spent the next decade trying to pretend it wasn't a workable strategy until Japanese economic performance (based on these principles) convinced them this wasn't going away.

Continuous quality improvement (usually abbreviated "CQI") incorporates several fundamental concepts:

1. <u>Testing doesn't create quality</u>: As someone who worked on pharmaceutical company projects where they'd tripled the quality control headcount with rework/scrappage/ defective product returns increasing every step of the way, I've seen this one up close. Quality needs to be built in – with better processes – not enforced after the fabrication. It's driven by workers, not overseers.

2. <u>Quality isn't won with a single flashy victory</u>: Successful quality programs aren't flashy; there's never a point where you stand on the aircraft carrier with the "Mission Accomplished" banner. That's because the mission's never accomplished. You can always get better, get smarter, and do more with less.

3. <u>Quality processes must change as the world changes</u>: Regulations will change. Customer demands will change. Your workforce will change and your production line will age … Your processes must adapt to these changes if you're going to continue producing quality goods and services.

Most successful quality initiatives today are driven by the Deming/Juran thinking rather than their original programs. These systems usually have several elements in common:

They minimize variation

- Mistakes and quality problems creep in when there's lots of room for error. Effective quality initiatives make sure the production processes are consistent. This DOESN'T MEAN you're static. You can isolate a problem and fix it if you have a bad process that's consistent – but you have no idea what element (or series of elements) is causing difficulties if there's too much variation in the process.

- They use standardized work processes. This means that all elements of the process are documented and tracked so management's aware of what happens at each step. Again, this does NOT mean that the process is carved in stone. Changes should be made, but they've got to be made in a way that's consistent and fully understood or management will, once again, be groping for black felines in the anthracite storage at midnight. You can make changes every hour on the hour so long as the changes are documented and the results are tracked.

- The work process is broken into defined cells. This is NOT mass production. It's ensuring that actions are happening in small, discrete elements where their outcome can be tracked and skills can be built.

- Work output is also tracked in specific batches. This is critical for quality issues. A common managerial error is to allow mixing of new processing and re-work; this eliminates problem tracing for all of the final input, and can cause serious customer problems if you ever have a product recall.

They increase throughput

- Too many shop floor managers assume that they need to "crack the whip" because workers are lazy and unmotivated. In fact, an assumption of poor motivation becomes a self-fulfilling prophecy: people who are treated like idiots will live up to your expectations. The findings of Toyota, of GE, of Procter & Gamble and many others are that employees who are treated as responsible partners end up acting responsibly.

- There's a common fiction that supervisors' "pushing shipments out the door" actually increases shipments out the door.In fact, it often increases scrap and re-work, which ultimately slows down the process of getting the specified goods to the customer right and on time.

- High throughput is a function of improving the weakest link. Practically, this may create its own "Domino Effect"-style cascade of problems, when you fix one major glitch and find you had several other smaller ones that stayed hidden until your first fix raised throughput enough to see the smaller issues. Expect it and work through it.

Frederick W. Croft

- High throughput is a function of smarts, skill and knowledge. It's not a function of intensity.

These are some high level characteristics. Let's take a look at some of the common approaches to consider some of the specifics. We'll begin at the beginning.

SIX SIGMA

Let's go for some word association, shall we? How about "Six Sigma successes"? We get ourselves some "Jack Welch," some "Southwest Airlines," some "Larry Bossidy," some "GE" and "Honeywell" and "Emerson." We get "world class performance" and "backbone of competitive excellence."

Okay, how about "Six Sigma failures"? Shazam, we get "US auto industry." We get "health care"; we get "70% of the projects get scrapped without yielding anything." In several cases, we get "state government."

Obviously, Six Sigma isn't a simple subject, and we won't find any simple analyses when we examine it. Let's take a closer look what Six Sigma is trying to do, and how it goes about doing it.

Six Sigma is a method of controlling variation *and tracking your own performance as you do so.* Six Sigma is disciplined and scientific about all of this, so the process includes two of the most dreaded words in the English language: math and statistics. The good news is that, with spreadsheets and other aids, the numbers part of this isn't too difficult for the average user.

Let's think about performance over a group of operations. Sometimes things will go better than others. Usually, this ends up spreading over one of those Bell curves you recall from high school:

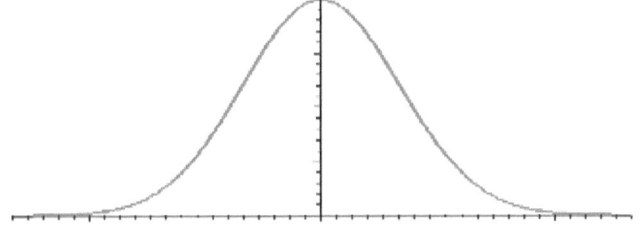

Performance goes from the really fantastic at the left to the truly abysmal on the right, but the majority of entries – around two-thirds – are clustered right around the midpoint of the graph. This is true regardless of what you're measuring. When looking at variation, statisticians are looking at what portion of the results ends up within ranges in the curve.

Of course, noting the shape of the curve reminds us of the "fat tailed" curve we looked at earlier. Six Sigma assumes that the distribution is Gaussian (i.e., follows the Bell curve). If reality doesn't match the assumption, you're results won't, either (*vide* the eventual results of the Bell curve-based Li formula which was used to build all those CDO bond issues that blew up in the Great Worldwide Meltdown). This is a fundamental issue that gets overlooked in too many Six Sigma training sessions (since too many of these are handled by trainers, not people who've actually managed production …) Six Sigma processes can and do work, but "trust, but verify" remains a requirement.

For the moment, let's assume we've really got a Gaussian distribution and that the Six Sigma method will match reality. We're usually only looking at a part of the whole range when we're looking at a curve distribution: the portion between the absolute minimum performance the customer will tolerate (the "lower satisfaction limit," or "LSL") and the best performance that we can afford to give the customer for the sale price (the "upper satisfaction limit," or "USL"):

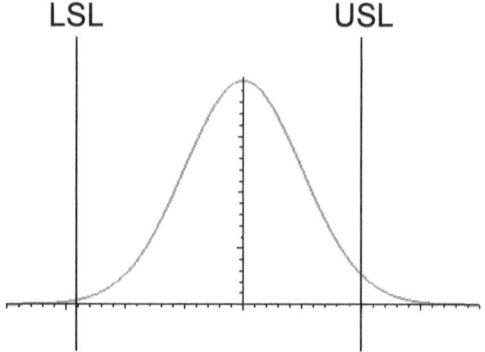

The size of this range determines how much variation we're willing to live with. Each range element is called a "standard deviation" (i.e., the amount it deviates from the midpoint or "mean"). This standard deviation range is abbreviated as "Sigma" (σ) because statistical types love to use Greek letters to show how damn technical they are. Depending on how many standard deviations you insist on, there can be a wide shift in the number of mistakes you're willing to accept:

σ	Defects per Million	Percentage Yield
2	308,537	69.15%
3	66,807	93.32%
4	6,210	99.38%

σ	Defects per Million	Percentage Yield
5	233	99.98%
6	3.4	99.99%

With two standard deviations, roughly 31 defects out of every one hundred would be unacceptable. By three standard deviations you only have 6.7 problems out of every hundred, and by the time you get to the Six Sigma level (six standard deviations) you're down to 3.4 problems out of one million. The average business starts out somewhere around two sigma, so we're looking at an improved quality goal on the order of ten thousand times.

The idea here is that the business sets a goal of holding defects down to 3.4 parts per million: the Six Sigma level. Lower defects will result in happier customers, lower defect and rework costs, and other good things as we pointed out above. And happier customers is a basic focus of the Six Sigma process; there is a priority set on identifying "the Voice of the Customer" through ongoing communication processes, and using said Voice to guide your efforts. "Defects" are customer-defined, not decreed by management.

But, as is usually the case when some bright lad figures out how to spin straw into gold – there is a price to be paid, and the sinister Rumplestilskin will show up to collect it.

In the case of Six Sigma, the price is your corporate soul: Six Sigma requires you to live the life and believe the beliefs:

- Strong and passionate leadership that will support

the program and won't accept failure.
- A clear focus on measurable returns and numerically-driven decision-making.
- A willingness to wait for results: most Six Sigma efforts take two to three years.
- A commitment to driving decisions with verifiable data rather than best practices, opinions or guesswork.
- A special caste of experts – "Champions," "Master Black Belts" or "Senseis," etc. – to lead and implement the project.

Six Sigma isn't a casual exercise. You're putting everything you've got on the line. This makes it a pretty difficult process to start cold.

Let's Talk About These Experts

Experts drive Six Sigma. Some people love the concept of getting more and better certifications and becoming incredibly marketable and well-paid, so the notion of "belts" is really appealing to some of your staff. Others distrust the whole "cult" aspect of it, and worry that, if they join the program, they'll wake up one morning and find themselves chanting and eating brown rice. Neither concept has much to do with the expert "belt" roles in Six Sigma.

Six Sigma relies on qualified experts to facilitate for several reasons:

- Six Sigma uses technical concepts (operational and statistical) where a good instructor and guide is needed to get them across to line employees.

- Six Sigma projects are long term initiatives aimed

at changing corporate culture; they often take eighteen months to two years. It's hard to lead that type of effort on an ad hoc basis.

These needs pushed Six Sigma into developing a cadre of experts filling different roles in the effort and having different skill sets. These include:

"Sponsor": The high level executive responsible for securing the support necessary for the project's success. This person doesn't need to be a Six Sigma expert, but will:

- Work with Six Sigma professionals to develop the project charter.
- Provide counsel throughout the project
- Make sure the project's viewpoint and needs are represented at the top levels of the company.
- Attend out-briefs.

"Champions": Champions usually operate at a high level to ensure alignment between the overall business goals and specific Six Sigma initiatives. A Champion should have a solid Six Sigma background, and will participate in:

- Guiding the Project selection process
- Establishing decision guidelines for the Six Sigma methodology
- Providing mentoring and guidance to Master Black Belts and Black Belts
- Reallocating work to allow for growth opportunities
- Project reviews
- Search for new opportunities and possibilities

"Master Black Belt": Master Black Belts normally head up Six Sigma drives for larger companies, overseeing multiple projects and setting the tone for the company's efforts. They:

- Partner with project leaders and help them transform culture and deliver business results.
- Are consultants and strategy planning partners to project leaders
- Are developers of new ideas and techniques

"Black Belt": This is a full time role for a leader who runs projects and trains/mentors the other projects staff in Six Sigma issues and activities. The role includes:

- Trainer
- Mentor to Green Belts
- Tracks progress against strategic goals

"Green Belt": These are trained staff people who form the core of the project teams. They work with production staff in a number of ways:

- Culture transformation
- Help the team develop new approaches
- Help the team achieve productivity gains
- Track team performance

The Belt process is not different than CPA or IEEE designations: it indicates who has the skill base to do what – or at least who passed a test purporting to verify said skill base. But it means the company either (a.) is going to take bucketloads of time to get employees trained, or (b.) has to spend additional dollars recruiting employees who are already trained. Six Sigma has been around long enough that there are considerable numbers of people with Six Sigma belts in the work force, but there is always a human resources cost for certifications (to say nothing of the confusion issues that any type of certification can cause ...).

<u>The Six Sigma Process</u>

Six Sigma involves quite a few specific processes and techniques, most of which are beyond the scope of this discussion. All of these are, in turn, driven and managed by statistical tests which verify the extent to which problems are or aren't happening and solutions are or aren't working. There are several overriding implications which emerge from all this:

1. MANAGING VARIATION IS A STATISTICAL PROCESS

DMAIC

The various tests in Six Sigma all track progress from a starting point. This requires that the starting point (the "current state" that we discussed earlier) be mapped and measured in detail. It also requires that changes be introduced and monitored through a systematic process.

The process used in Six Sigma is known as "DMAIC":

Define
Measure
Analyze
Improve/Implement

Control

It works like this:

Define: Identify the actual problem, and the specific elements which create it. This is followed by a definition of the future state: what does it look like when the problem's totally solved and we've reached the Age of Aquarius? "Identify" and "definition" are driven by actual, verifiable and quantifiable measures; we're not talking about opinions or adjectives.

Measure: This refers both to the actual components – metrics and statistical confidence and all that – and to the information you can derive from relationships between the numbers. What are the key (80 – 20) items in all your information?
What do they tell you about (a.) the relationship between components, and (b.) the root cause of problems? This process also helps you prioritize problems and determine where the initial resolutions efforts get focused.

Analyze: Now you're finally ready to do something intelligent about the problem. Six Sigma's statistical and process tools are applied to the problem to devise potential solutions. Root cause analysis is critical here: if your solution only addresses surface issues, the deeper (unresolved) problems will continue to throw monkeywrenches in the proverbial machinery.

Improve/Implement: Great ideas don't count; great solutions do. To go beyond defining the solution to having the problem actually solved requires follow-up, tracking measurements, a ability to stay focused on the problem in spite of crises du jour and other distractions, and a thick skin to endure the whining and abuse aimed in your direction when everyone realizes that you're really serious and will be annoying enough to insist on results. You won't succeed unless you're willing to be disliked, since the people who aren't performing don't like to perform – and won't like you when you force them to perform.

Control: If you can't measure it, you can't manage it. Specific, numerical performance statistics have to be tracked at frequent intervals. They also need to be published at regular intervals – peer pressure is a great motivator. This is a recognition issue, not an economic one. Positive reinforcements (memos, pizza parties, whatever) emphasize to line employees (a.) that they really can – and did – do this stuff, and (b.) that good things will result when problems are solved. But, to be honest, the biggest motivators are the ugly, negative ones that drove GE's performance: there will be consequences for your job if you don't accept the program and meet your commitments.

About now, you're probably thinking that this has a definite family resemblance to that Scientific Method stuff we talked about earlier, and you're right. It's another flavor of the same thing. As noted above, this is an approach that has consistently worked since Sir Isaac Newton was dodging apple bombardments.

Six Sigma Won't Work Without Information
This is a technique that needs numbers. Lots of numbers. No statistics equals no statistical analysis equals your Six Sigma project dead in the water.

This is where most of those seventy percent who never make it walk into the wall: they can't force themselves to get organized enough and systematic enough to accumulate the data elements that are needed.

Six Sigma Drives the Company With Numbers

It needs quantitative thinking throughout the company. Six Sigma doesn't go for hunches, intuition, judgment, spirit messages, or Ouija Boards. You need to be able to explain, defend – and, hopefully, understand – your processes.

Six Sigma spends much time giving employees tools to attack problems. Some of these are quite simple. A basic tool in Six Sigma is the "5 Whys" process. This is a method that's apparently extracted from that tiresome old nursery rhyme about "for want of a nail, the kingdom was lost". The principle is simple: for every problem component, you ask "why" and keep on asking until you've either arrived at the root cause or been bludgeoned into unconsciousness for being such an insufferable little twerp.

EXAMPLE

Problem: You are on your way home from work and your car stops in the middle of the road.

1. Why did your car stop?
- *Because it ran out of gas.*
2. Why did it run out of gas?
- *Because I didn't buy any gas on my way to work.*
3. Why didn't you buy any gas this morning?
- *Because I didn't have any money.*
4. Why didn't you have any money?
- *Because I lost it all last night in a poker game.*
5. Why did you lose your money in last night's poker game?
- *Because I'm not very good at bluffing when I don't have a good hand.*

There's nothing magic about repeating the process five times: the presumption is that five repetitions is likely to get you to the root cause without pushing the other team members over the edge to homicide.

Having found the root cause and developed a proposed solution, you then shift into classic lab science mode and try out the solution while carefully observing and measuring the results. The results then lead you to other issues: you re-tune your analysis and run the process one more time.

Another common Six Sigma approach is an Ishikawa Diagram, usually referred to as a "fishbone diagram" for reasons that are self-evident when you look at one. The fishbone diagram defines causes for your problem. The concern here is "root cause analysis": finding those deeper problems which ultimately affect company performance.

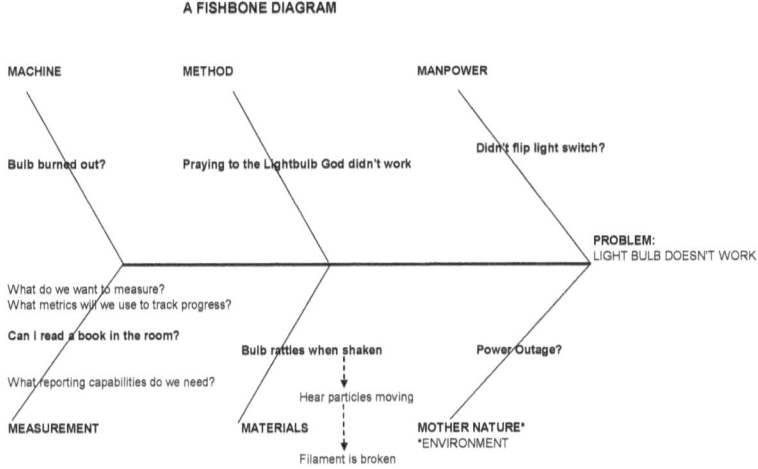

A FISHBONE DIAGRAM

We've identified a problem: we've got a light bulb that doesn't work. This is certainly a problem, but it's not yet actionable. We're not sure what to do in order to fix it.

The fishbone diagram suggests that we look at six areas:

1. <u>Manpower</u>: Is this a problem caused by poor training or the wrong people on the job (i.e., all those old jokes about how many *[fill in the societal subgroup to be slandered here]* it takes to change a light bulb)? Do we have enough people to accomplish the task according to the requirements?

2. <u>Method</u>: What have we done to address the problem in the past, and why didn't that work? Where are we buying those bulbs again – and should we transport them in a better way than dragging the bag down the street? Did we neglect standard maintenance, calibration, or other basic issues that could've prevented the problem? Are people assigned the right tasks?

3. <u>Machine</u>: Is this a machinery problem? Is it the bulb or the socket? If so, is this old and tired equipment – or am I using a hammer for a job that requires a PC?

4. <u>Measurement</u>: Do we know what we're measuring when we say we've got a problem? Is the bulb dim, or dead?

5. <u>Materials</u>: Is this an issue caused by poor raw stock or shoddy workmanship? (Buying those cheap bulbs again …) In our illustration, we see how following up with clarifying questions helps us drill down to the final issue: the rattle in the bulb tells us that we've got a broken filament, and (since a broken filament interrupts the circuit) we now know why our light bulb isn't going on.

6. <u>Mother Nature</u>
<u>(the Environment</u>: There are problems caused by

factors beyond our control.
(If the power went out, the bulb could still be fine …)
If that's the case, we need to know that.

Once the problem has been identified, efforts can be focused on creating a sustainable solution. This can be:

1. A corrective action: An action taken to eliminate the root cause of a nonconformity, defect or other problem that has already taken place, or

2. A preventive action: An action taken to eliminate the cause of a potential nonconformity, defect or other problem which hasn't happened yet to keep it from ever taking place.

With these tools, and with all the various other Six Sigma approaches, the idea is to follow the DMAIC approach, develop hypotheses with a reasonable chance of addressing the problem, and test them to see if they work.

Everybody Plays

This is an approach that needs analytic skills AT ALL LEVELS. Six Sigma pushes decision making down to the production floor where the majority of the problems happen. Executive micromanagement doesn't work in a Six Sigma environment – which is an issue that has to be worked through in its implementation.

2. MANAGING VARIATION IS AN EXECUTIVE AND SHAREHOLDER COMMITMENT

Six Sigma is a two-year process. DMAIC and Culture

Change take time. In a world filled with securities markets clamoring for quarterly results and banks auditing clients on 90-day centers, taking two years to see if it worked is a pretty tough sell. The companies that have gotten the results have been the ones with executives – the Jack Welches or Larry Bossidys – who were tough enough while being persuasive enough to keep the short term world away from their throats long enough for their long term initiative to work.

A number of practitioners, notably Deming himself, have approached this as a faith-based process: you need to place your trust in the method, pay no attention to financial analyses or other tools from outside the process, and fight through in the sure and certain knowledge that the system will eventually work its magic.

This has a disturbing resemblance to the "stay the course" approaches discussed above. And, for those of us who require the co-operation of bankers, shareholders and other annoying types, it works about as well as "stay the course" did in Iraq.

3. MANAGING VARIATION IS A COMMUNICATIONS PROCESS

This is that "voice of the Customer" stuff we mentioned earlier. In Six Sigma a "customer" isn't just a purchaser: they're any person (inside your company or outside) who receives your goods and/or services at any step in the process.

Six Sigma recognizes that lone heroes don't accomplish much in larger organizations; success requires team performance. Effective teams, in turn require a common direction, co-ordination, problem alerts and other reflexes that don't "just happen." Six Sigma's construction around statistical-performance measures only increases the need for effective communications systems, since most folks in line/production roles won't have a solid background in math, systems or finance.

Six Sigma includes a number of communications approaches designed to address this problem. Many of these are visual, using the "picture is worth a thousand words" school of leadership to diagram out concepts that aren't easy to describe verbally.

Some of the common visual approaches in Six Sigma include:

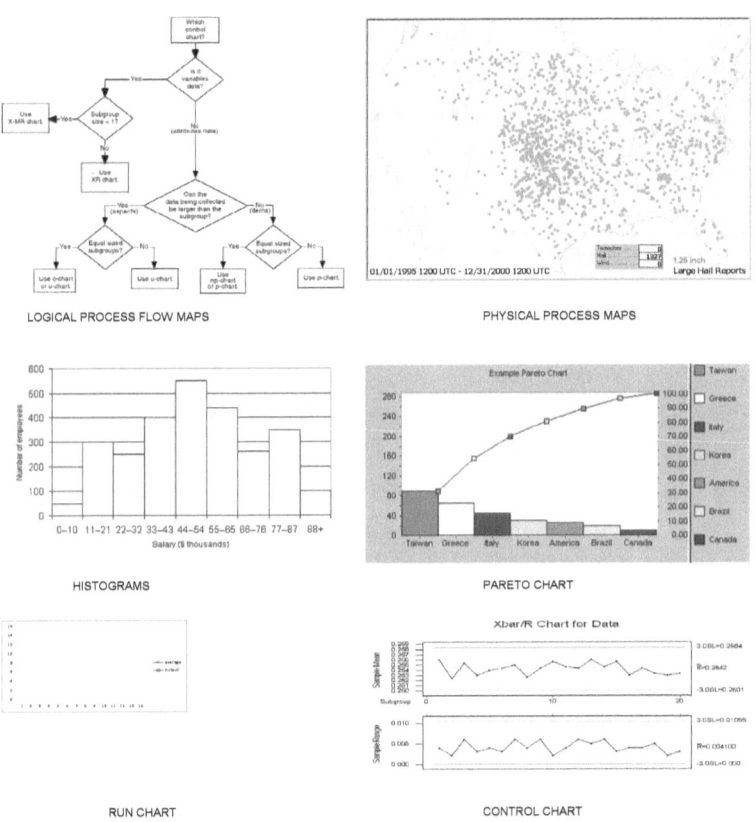

LOGICAL PROCESS FLOW MAPS

PHYSICAL PROCESS MAPS

HISTOGRAMS

PARETO CHART

RUN CHART

CONTROL CHART

With visual tools, everyone sees and understands the measurements being used to manage the operations. This requirement for common and immediate visibility also affects the methods used to circulate the visual data.

One of the key movements in current manufacturing management is visual factory initiatives. These offer several advantages:

- They reduce search time
- They eliminate questions
- They improve safety around shipping or equipment environments
- They improve communication
- They improve employee satisfaction in the workplace

The classic application of this is through the "Visual Factory." The theory is simple: there are large graphic displays at each section of the shop floor. They show staging: what projects are on time, what projects are lacking, how many units are in stock, what's in the production queue, and so forth. Ideally, these displays are digital, so they can re-set on a real time basis:

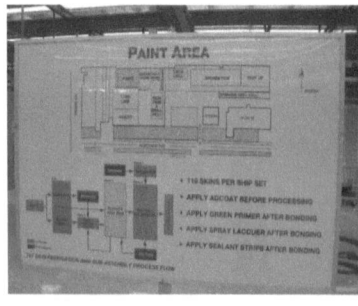 

In addition to ensuring that all parties understand what is happening at a given time, the visual shop floor approach provides motivation to workers (since times that they're slow or have problems become publicly visible).

The goal with all of these communication methods is to create an execution-focused dialogue that is:

- Continuous, and

- Ongoing

WHAT IN THE WORLD EVER HAPPENED TO SIX SIGMA?

So why the $&*@!!!! Isn't everyone doing this?

Like all transformational ideas, Six Sigma has generated its share of controversy. The frequently-cited one is an analysis by someone named Charles Holland (from a consulting firm called QualPro which uses a different process). Holland's study stated that, of 58 large companies that announced Six Sigma programs, 91% had performance that trailed the Fortune 500 since the announcement. Holland's study has been disputed by other analysts, and details of his work haven't been published or vetted. One could also note that performance lag immediately after the announcement may be a result of performance issues that motivated Six Sigma adoption in the first place, rather than an aspect of Six Sigma itself ... But concerns about process effectiveness remain.

Beyond this, several commentators – notably J. M. Juran – claim that there's nothing new in Six Sigma, and most of its tools have been imported, or adapted and slightly tweaked, from other programs. There's some truth in this, but I'm not sure why that's a problem for the manager using it to get performance improvements. Six Sigma has been unapologetic about taking the best ideas out there and integrating them into the methodology. This is one of its strengths.

The biggest issue I've seen is translating Six Sigma knowledge into action. We've seen a lot of companies who staffed up on Black Belts, but didn't give them management support.Problems are identified, but the forces of inertia keep changes from happening.

The way around this is, unfortunately, the Jack Welch Special: you make sure that people who don't work the program and meet their commitments have career disappointments.

THE BOTTOM LINE

1. Six Sigma can work extremely well, and has made major contributions to the performance of world-class Fortune 1000 companies.

2. This doesn't happen automatically. In order to succeed, it requires:

- Real CEO/Board-level commitment
- An existing technical/quantitative environment that can manage using numbers
- A data infrastructure that can support the process.
- Time to train and implement.
- A shareholder and capital infrastructure that can support a multi-year transformational process.

3. If your actual risk differs from the Bell curve assumption, your actual results will vary from the Six Sigma calculations, and need to be tweaked accordingly.

LEAN (TOYOTA MANUFACTURING SYSTEM)

Six Sigma isn't the only approach to create process/ execution improvement. The Japanese efforts that created US interest in improved management systems were based on a very different approach. The method they came up with is generally referred to as "Lean" (although some sources refer to it as "Toyota Manufacturing System," since Shigeo Shingo and Taiichi Ohno, the Japanese production executives who developed many of the concepts, did so while working for Toyota). Where Six Sigma focuses on controlling variation, Lean achieves its results through management of waste.

WASTE

There's a lot of inefficiency in the world. The "rule of thumb" (which is in quotation marks so you'll remember to stay suspicious of non-documented statistics) states that fifty percent of the time and effort in most corporations is spent on actions that don't accomplish anything: walking around, problem discussions that don't produce a solution, papershuffling so someone can cover their ass ... Lean refers to this stuff as "Non-Value Added," and there's an insane amount of it out there:

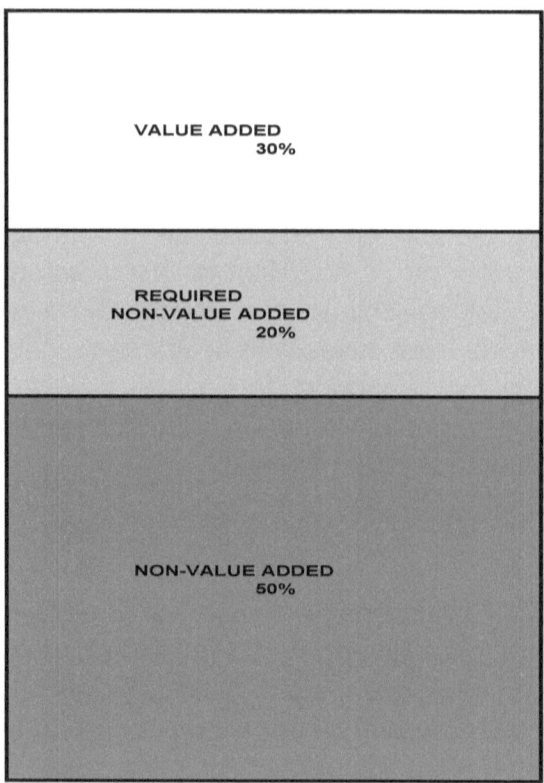

If these standard "rules of thumb" are right, 70% of what we're doing is a waste of time. Some of it you're stuck with ("necessary non-value added" includes processes required by regulations, which don't add to the bottom line but do have costs). But much of it (referred to as "non-value added" in the vernacular) can be removed with better practices in operations.

Lean's focus on "waste" is, at its core, a focus on results. Customers don't WANT paperwork: they want quality or information. They don't WANT re-work: they want the results that they purchased goods or services from you to accomplish. But many organizations find "results" a peripheral, somewhat threatening concept.

The guys who came up with Lean find all of this "non-value added," "waste" stuff deeply, personally offensive. Japan, where all of this originated, is the place where they invented Minimalism: a flower arrangement is one flower in a vase in an otherwise empty room. Less is more.

Sure, Lean is about "removing waste in corporate operations." But it's more than that. It's a way to make things simpler. More understandable. More elegant and graceful.

"Waste" is an interesting concept in Japanese. Where English uses a single word, Japanese has three words for "waste":

1. *Muda* – Any activity that's non-productive or doesn't add value. *Muda* occurs when more goods and services than necessary are used to produce a product, even if the product is something that the customer actually wants. There's a moral and aesthetic component to quality – and an ugliness to lack of quality.

2. *Mura* – Any unevenness or inconsistency, either in physical objects or in the human spiritual condition. Again, value isn't simply defined in terms of output but is the product of an aesthetic process. (The concern about inconsistency reminds us of Six Sigma's desire for consistent output ...)

3. *Muri* – An unreasonableness, overburdening or absurdity.

The Japanese have studied all the ways you can expend energy without getting anywhere. They find them ugly and embarrassing. "Waste," in this view, is a larger issue than a simple failure to execute. It's personal failure.

In Lean, the goal is for removal of "waste" to be a part of life, a practice, a moral commitment. Those readers who've studied a martial art may have run across a phrase: "moving meditation." The idea behind moving meditation is that, when you get good enough at a practice or *way*, the execution isn't something you think through but is something that arises spontaneously as an expression of your deepest spiritual self. It's part of you. You're not some jerk following the steps; you're living your *art*. The goal in Lean, like the goal in martial arts, becomes to get beyond the discipline to the reflexive, the instinctive.

Ultimately, this is very real world and very practical, however much it sounds like the old dude Darryl Hannah kills off in *Kill Bill*. Lean is about doing more with less:

- Less time
- Less space
- Less materials
- Less machinery
- Less human effort

THE EIGHT WASTES

One of the great virtues of Lean is that it's really simple: it gives you a few concepts and a couple of lists to remind you of what's important. This has several advantages for the company:

a. <u>You can implement fast</u> – We've gotten initial results in as little as 90 days with Lean. A full Six Sigma initiative often takes several years, but Lean can start paying for itself in a quarter or so.

b. <u>It's easy to understand</u> – You don't need to be Einstein to handle Lean. No statistics; not much study. This makes it easier to convince nervous line employees, and allows them to make use of the principles quickly. There's less for them to screw up.

c. <u>It gives everyone a common language</u> – With Lean, the CEO and the janitor are looking at the same issues. There's not much confusion; everyone knows what's expected, and everyone has a concept "toolkit" that they can use to solve problems and create results.

The Eight Wastes are a basic tool in Lean. They're just what they sound like. They're eight business elements. They're wasteful. And they're really common:

THE EIGHT WASTES

<u>1. Over Production:</u>
You make stuff that is never used; you start projects that are never finished; you make too much. Examples might be preparing extra copies of reports that no one uses; work that goes into projects that are abandoned; extra stuff that never makes it onto the shop floor or is made and never sold.

<u>2. Re-Work:</u>
A war story. A few years ago we were working on cost analysis at a bakery, and one of the questions that came up was how much scrap was adding to our production expense. No one had thought much about it. So we asked to see the current week's scrap. Eight forty-foot dumpsters, for four days' excess. You could've filled

every house on my block with the scrap bread that was being tossed weekly (though I'd prefer it if you didn't ...). Tossed bread equals tossed dollars.

Another war story. We were working with a vitamin manufacturer. Thirty percent of their production runs were sent back to be re-worked; and twenty percent went through re-work three or four times. The interesting thing about this was that they felt it was a good sign: it showed they "were serious about quality."

I made a comment earlier: You can't inspect in quality. This is a realization that comes from LOTS of real world input. Quality goes in as part of the process, or it never gets in at all. You can't bolt it on after the fact like a bumper. That famous story about Toyota – how they showed they were serious by allowing anyone in the plant to stop the production line if they saw a problem – was really just a story about the Japanese accepting reality. Their beancounters weren't any happier about stoppages than anyone else's, *but they recognized that it's cheaper to fix it now than postponing it until the end.* You'll get quality if you build it in as a basic part of the process, and you'll make money when you do:

QUALITY = EFFICIENCY = PROFITS

3. Inventory:
We were involved in acquisition integration for a private equity firm a few years back, a division of a larger company that had been bought and was going to run independently. Since the buyer was re-financing as part of the acquisition, we went to look at things we could use as collateral, inventory being one of them. And we found what you always find when you look at inventory: things were lost, things were obsolete, things were busted.

After $14 million in write-downs, we'd nailed down the inventory number.

This happens every damn time you look at inventory. Many people think of inventory as "a safety factor," but I've never had any of them explain to me why having an "asset" that's ALWAYS going to cost you money and still not be there when you really need it is a good idea. It's not safe to lose your net worth.

To make it more amazing, I've seen a surprising number of Controllers (who should know better) take the same position. After all, inventory gives them a borrowing base that can be used to pull money from the bank when cash gets tight ... Why paying interest to get back 50% on your asset is a good idea remains unexplained.

People think that having minimum inventory amounts is necessary for customer service. They're often wrong. We worked with a cell phone company where we moved inventory turns from 7 times annually to 24 times (which is easier than you'd think) and had no customer problems. In most companies a reduction of 70% in inventory costs racks up some serious savings ...

4. Processing:
We started this chapter noting all of the things that happen in a corporate environment that don't create a result: sign-offs, meaningless standards ... This
is the sort of thing that creates $800 toilet seats for military procurement – and it's not limited to the military.
Most people on the production line can tell you how things are done. What they can't tell you is WHY they're done. If you find processes that are traditional rather than results-focused, this is a good time to turn the Nike slogan around and "Just DON'T do it."

5. Motion:

I was recently in a vitamin plant where raw materials were stored in lockers near the loading dock. When material went into production, it was taken in handcarts from the lockers to an area about thirty yards away where the impurities were sifted out.After that, it was taken (again, in handtrucks) another fifty yards away where the materials were combined together to make a production blend. The blends were then trucked another twenty yards where they were loaded into an encapsulation machine. The machine jammed easily, so four of the line guys were climbing over the machine and smoothing out the blend by hand so it would go through without creating a blockage. At the far end of the machine, the capsules drop into individual bottles. The bottling machine didn't work so hot, so a crew of line guys grab each bottle as it comes through the machine and hand-twist the caps to make sure that they're on tight.

The bottles are sold in four-packs, so the bottles from each production run are then moved about ten yards away and stacked to wait for the other three types of production to be run. Once that happens, someone runs out to the plant to round up everyone in the area. They then move piles of these bottles to the open section of the staging room (about twenty yards) and start assembling them into four-packs. The packs are then loaded onto handtrucks and carted back to the shipping dock on the other side of the building.

You were going to do better on the production line if you lettered in track in high school.

Companies spend a lot of time moving stuff. The *stuff* in question can get damaged or lost during this process, and the employees involved in stuff-movement create little value for their effort other than aerobic exercise.

Less moves and less hand-offs mean less time, less personnel cost and less screw-ups.

Motion also takes space. In a production facility, space is the final cost frontier: you're paying for every square foot. If things are more organized and closer together, this frees up space which can be sub-leased, turned back to the building owner, or otherwise converted from an unnecessary drain to a profit center.

6. Transport:
The same thing that happens inside the facility happens in the world at large.

One of our auto aftermarket clients had 36 warehouses located all over the United States. Each of them needed basic inventory; each of them needed trucking to get the inventory to and from them. When they took a look at what was really needed, this got reduced to four. Companies with international fabrication face this problem in every step of the production process: getting stuff manufactured in one place; getting it moved overland to the port; getting it cleared through customs and sent to the fulfillment house; getting it from the fulfillment house to the customer. Every step in this journey is an extra cost, and every step another node where things can go wrong.

7. Waiting:
The mantra of the Army used to be "Hurry up and wait." That's an expensive mantra. Time not only is money, it COSTS money. Interest costs are a function of time you borrow the money: if it takes you an extra week to get paid because the product was sitting around waiting for that one component somebody forgot to order, that's a week of bank charges that could've been avoided if people were paying attention.

8. Confusion:
Many people in Lean talk about "Seven Wastes," and this is the one they leave off. In my experience, this is the most expensive of all. When one hand doesn't know what the other one is doing, the odds are that they're both in your wallet extracting dollars that will get thrown out the window.

6S METHODS

In addition to pointing out things that cause waste, Lean has plenty of tools and specific methods to get rid of waste in your work environment. One of the major ones consists of six tools cleverly called "6 S" because there are six of them, and (wait for it!) they all begin with "S":

1. Sorting: This refers to the process of going through the tools and equipment in the work environment and only keeping what you need. Everything else is stored or discarded.

2. Straightening: The idea here is to arrange tools and equipment so it will be as easy as possible to do the job. Normally, this means they're set in the order they will be used and located convenient to the flow path of the projects.

3. Sweeping: Cleanliness – and restoring the work environment so it stays organized – should be a part of daily work, not something that happens when everyone gets around to calling the cleaning staff. Everything should be restored to its place at the end of the day, and the work site should be supplied, cleaned and ready to go for the next time that it's used.

4. <u>Standardizing</u>: We spoke earlier about the importance of creating consistent performance that can then be tuned to achieve optimum results. Understanding your "current state – knowing exactly what happens from the time you receive a customer inquiry to your delivery of the finished goods – is a fundamental for Lean, and a requirement for effective production.

5. <u>Sustaining</u>: Life goes on after the heroic charge up San Juan Hill. The organization needs to maintain and review standards to prevent backsliding.

6. <u>Safety</u>: It's considered unproductive to kill off your employees.

6S is about getting organized:

FROM THIS

TO THIS

6 S isn't maintenance. It's a method of keeping Lean current, making it a part of daily work rather than a concept in a seminar. It's also a means of strengthening signal/output by minimizing noise in the environment.

EFFECTIVE EFFORT

The concept of "standard volume" goes back to Alfred Sloan: you set up the classic mass production line and keep a steady stream of work going down it until the stuff emerges at the end. This is a great concept if your idea of Paradise is a zombie army producing mountains of crap nobody wants. It's not effective.

Lean looks at production in a different way. It focuses on creating products as they're needed, managing the process through a concept called "takt time" for no reason that I've been able to discover. (It's either German for "heartbeat" or Japanese for "the average amount of time we need to get this piece of crap out the door.")

The idea with takt time is to only staff your production with the people you need to do the jobs you've got right now. Rather than building a bunch of junk whether or not anyone's asked for it, you only produce the stuff where you've got actual orders in hand. You drive fabrication according to "pull" (an order showing the product is needed) rather than "push" (a forecast cooked up by somebody with an MRP system and never tied back to real needs).

It's driven by the rate your customers buy your product. The minutes of needed work that can be produced in a day divided by the number of units needed for that day equal the takt time.

Let's look at a working example:

EXAMPLE:
A sales distribution company receives 340 orders per day for a product.

6 sales people are required to process the orders.

The company is in operation for 1 shift (7 hrs with breaks/lunch) and is trying to stick to 5 days per week.

CALCULATION

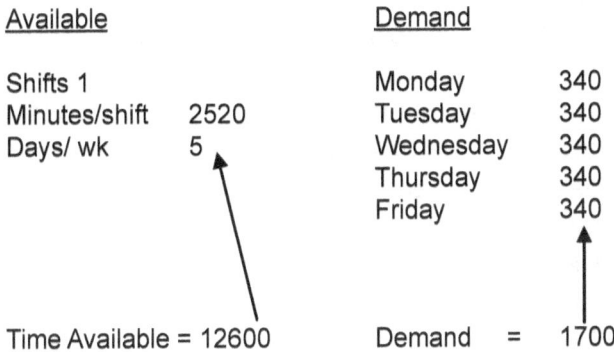

Available		Demand	
Shifts 1		Monday	340
Minutes/shift	2520	Tuesday	340
Days/ wk	5	Wednesday	340
		Thursday	340
		Friday	340
Time Available = 12600		Demand = 1700	

1. Determine the time available
2. Determine the demand for the period under review
3. Calculate Takt = Available time / Demand (A/D)

Average time
Demand   = 7.41 minutes

Once you've got the Takt time, you can then figure out how much of your workforce is idle or underused and deploy them accordingly: have them produce something else, send them to open up a new market, have them clean the place up ...   Just DON'T have them use up materials, machine time, utilities and all the rest to do stuff that doesn't need doing.

Only produce what you KNOW you need. This avoids excess inventory, overproduction, excess motion and all that bad stuff we talked about when looking at Eight Wastes. Reducing batch sizes is a key component in avoiding excess inventory, warehousing capacity problems, and general confusion. Takt time provides a quick method of breaking batch sizes, smoothing work flow and minimizing unproductive employee time.

The great complication in all of this is production time. When your line gets that order, they have to create the product, which means they have to get the raw materials, which have to be shipped in beforehand … Production folks try to minimize these problems be using various automated systems and techniques usually referred to as "materials resource planning" (or "MRP"). MRP forecasts work about as well as the horoscope forecasts in your local paper. There's room for improvement.

Lean's response to MRP problems is something called *kanban* or "just in time." You have the absolute minimum stuff around so you can deliver; no "safety stock" or "cushions." If your company's large enough, you can shift part of the stocking and supply problem to vendors by guaranteeing to buy an annual amount, and then have the vendor commit to only supply you when the goods are called for by you, and store it at their facility until called for. If your vendor's smart, they'll build in some charge for this, but that charge won't be paid until you actually call for the goods' delivery – a clean form of off-balance sheet financing.

WHAT CAN YOU EXPECT FROM LEAN?

The short answer here is: you can expect what you put into it. In practice, we've seen committed Lean initiatives save between four and ten times the funds invested, with initial savings taking place in the first 90 days and substantial improvements in the first year. Quick results have been a major factor in the sweep of American business toward Lean – but the program (once again!) requires a serious commitment from the top of the corporation if it's going to deliver all of the well-publicized results.

VIII
EXECUTION: JUST DO IT

WHY DO WE STILL HAVE
PROBLEMS MANAGING PROCESS?

We've just discussed a small arsenal of compelling tools for process management. Yet companies across the globe continue to have serious problems with operations management. What's going on?

The uncertainty issues and global complications that we've discussed earlier throw large money wrenches into the machinery for operations execution. Just consider the impact of current business conditions on parts of Lean and Six Sigma:

Kanban: Just in time techniques assume that there's enough time for demand shift to flow through the production (and communication) process and alter MRP-based forecasting drivers. With short product lifecycles and more offshore production, that's not always the case.

We recently worked with a client in the consumer electronics industry. These folks are seeing product lifecycles on the rough order of ninety days, while the time it takes to transit the order to their Chinese manufacturer, the manufacturer to get allocations for high-demand parts, fabricate the goods, ship them across the Pacific, and get them through customs runs about sixty days. A small mistake in procurement and you're stuck with 50% more inventory than your market wants.

This isn't just a problem for consumer electronics. Fashion, toys ... Small mistakes equal big inventory writedowns.

Variation: Six Sigma, standardized work, and many other process management tools are often seen from a perspective of processes existing over an extended period. That's less common than it used to be. Inflection points happen regularly, shifting fundamental rules in the basic components of business operation:

- Markets
- Technologies
- Capital source requirements

Stable processes will be destabilized by shifts in any of these areas.

Waste: Efficiency is always a benefit to business. But it's harder to be efficient when you're forever figuring out what just happened and what you have to do to adapt. The signal to noise issues we discussed earlier apply here as well.

We need a set of tools that can move off of the shop floor and out into the world, helping executives address the globalized, information-poor environments where they're actually working.

WHAT'S THE NEW GAME PLAN?

The management approach that's often used to address these issues is one that came from another field where optimal solutions are uncertain, work is distributed at multiple sites, and deadlines are tight. This is computer programming. Programming started in military and academic circles of the Sixties where highly structured planning was all the fashion, but this was irretrievably derailed by the rise of microcomputers and the hacker movement:

Military  Hacker
Precision   Anarchy

The looser, hipper operating styles of the hacker elite became business as usual. Cisco's John Chambers (a techie, but someone working in the stodgy telcom equipment side of the field) refers to three key elements for organizations that are going to succeed in the years ahead:

1. **Smarts** (access to immediate relevant information)

2. **Skills** (people with market responsiveness, initiative, creativity, self-confidence, and belief in the Seven Deadly Warning Signals of Dumb Stuff)

3. **Flexibility** (organizations that are communicating, continuously learning, and have the courage to quickly cut loose projects that aren't working while pulling the trigger on those that might).

These are obviously departures from the waterfall project plan. In fact, they're departures from ANY project plan: they're ready-fire-aim raised to a whole new level. How does this actually work in a company?

Frederick W. Croft

Many tech companies drive software development from a project framework called "agile programming." Agile programming is based on several assumptions that fit pretty closely with the globalized, uncertain world we're seeing in other business operations:

- They believe that formalized, "waterfall plan" approaches only work when you know the whole solution you're trying to create. Programming starts from an assignment where the designers often have only a vague idea of how they're going to deliver the goods. This is a situation that lots of other executives in lots of other fields are facing.

- They believe that the formalized, "waterfall plan" approaches only work when you own the production floor. That's not the case when you've got global fabrication and multiple subcontractors – which is the situation many of us are facing.

- They believe that the formalized, "waterfall plan" approaches create a bureaucratic, top down environment that really good people won't tolerate. If the production process doesn't respect the key designers, they'll show that they don't respect the process by going to a more outcomes-focused environment.

AGILE OPERATIONS

Increasingly, executives in high-demand environments are moving to an approach derived from the hacker ethics of agile programming called, predictably enough, "Agile Operations." Agile Operations takes the concepts and translates them from the world of high performance coding to the distribution, retail, manufacturing, and service environments where most of us are managing.

Agile Operations is based on six functions which change the impact of Six Sigma, Lean, and most other management approaches:

1. <u>BREAK IT UP</u>:

Big, complex project plans are like any other big, complex system. They don't work very well. Agile breaks each project into small, bite-sized sub-projects. These are usually tasks that can be finished in less than one week; two to three days is common.

In the early stages of definition and problem-solving, the tool of choice is often a common Lean technique called "Kaizen." (This is a Japanese corruption of a Mandarin phrase, "gai shan," which means "good change" or "change for the better"). This is basically a system for organized, focused, team-based brainstorming and follow-through. The most frequently applied flavor is something called a "Kaizen Blitz," in which the parties involved work intensively to fix problems and improve their overall operation.

Kaizen addresses several goals:

  a. Eliminate waste and non-value added processes

  b. Train staff to be more effective

  c. Improve work flow

  d. Improve productivity, and

  e. Reduce stress

It's built around something called the Shewhart Cycle, or "PDCA": Plan – Do – Check – Act:

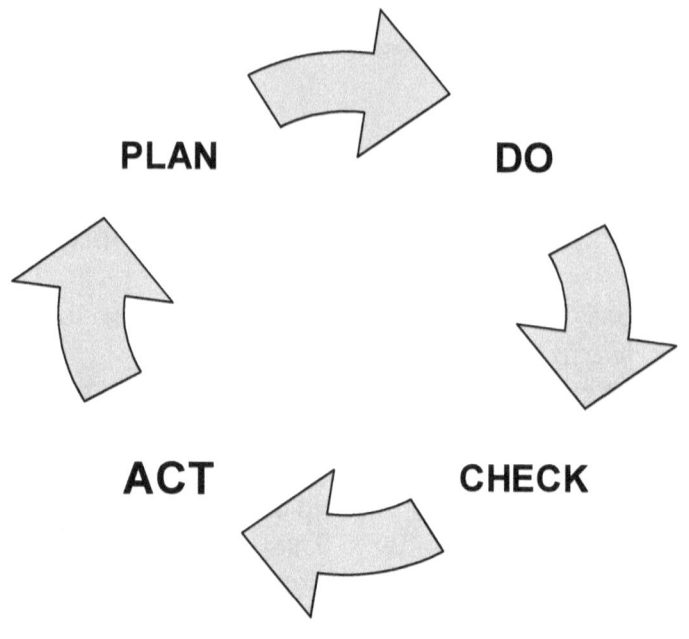

Each element of this four-step process involves multiple processes, ongoing collaboration, and mutual learning:

PLANNING

- Involves everyone. If it makes sense, this can include parties from outside the company (vendors, or even regulators).

- Addresses specific issues. This generally requires development of a team charter which documents the commitments of team members, the goals to be achieved, and the resources required.

- Requires measurements of relevant factors (i.e., scrap and re-work rates, routing of products, total distance products are moved in the factory, number and frequency of changeovers, worker time per staff, etc.)

- Often involves value stream mapping (flowcharting the materials flows, steps, activities, and other process elements involved in creating the product or service).

- Develops potential improvements using tools such as the Lean and Six Sigma procedures that we've discussed.

- Works to develop consensus about and ownership of a team-developed improvement. This includes milestone and critical path elements, as well as relevant performance statistics and expected performance factors. It also includes a review process, which can take place between two weeks and 90 days after the initial implementation, depending on the nature of the process.

DOING

- Post the consensus-agreed approach at the work site. People can't comply if they don't know what's expected.

- Staff executing the process must be trained. This will mean they need to understand the consensus-agreed approach to a standard process for the tasks. It often means they'll also need training in related concepts such as 6S.

- Methods of tracking need to be implemented using the agreed-upon performance statistics.

CHECKING

- Analyze statistical data collected and compare to expected factors.

- Variations are considered, and the processes where variations are produced are reviewed by team to understand why the variances occurred.

- The team then uses new data to develop revised procedures based on the observed actual performance. Revised statistics, milestones and critical path are developed

ACTING

- The revised approach is tested and tracked, with another follow-up.

This is yet another variation of our READY – FIRE – AIM approach, but it's one that takes place very quickly. Small, quick projects require close management attention. Focus is a key element here. Strategists from Clausewitz onward have described the need for concentrating forces on specific locations to ensure victory; the point remains valid in the present day.

There are quite a number of methods used for selecting the points of focus.

The most basic of these is that old standard, the

Telephone Number Rule, which states that you select the seven most important issues facing you at any point in time (seven being the number of digits in a basic telephone number, which supposedly is the maximum number of digits that the average person can keep in their head at any one time). You keep working on these, and, as you finish managing one, advance the next most important issue up so you're always working on the top seven at any point in time.

This raises the issue of just how you selected that top seven. The touch-stone that's been effective for me as an approach built on managing Showstoppers. A Showstopper is:

> An issue that can critically damage your project (or company, or asset, or job) if it doesn't work out correctly.

If you have more than seven of these at any one time, you might consider Dial-A-Prayer. If you've got a manageable number of these, you need to pay attention to them. While that seems to be an obvious statement, it's ignored quite regularly in the real world. We've had a startling number of clients who kept working on the simple issues because they were sources of quick victories (insert the obligatory quote about looking under the light for the keys lost in the darkness here) while the Showstoppers that ultimately killed the company were blithely ignored. Bad idea.

Showstoppers seldom get better when ignored. On several Boards of Directors where I've served, we've decided that the Board needed to examine the Ten Biggest Threats to the company on an annual basis:

Identify them
Quantify them
Prioritize Them
Develop Strategies for Addressing Them

This is not a recipe for popularity. It makes everyone nervous and means a lot of work for all concerned, since the Showstoppers (by definition) are the hardest issues the company faces and will take the most work to manage. But managing them beats the Hell out of the alternative, since sooner or later one of them will go wrong, at which point the Showstoppers are managing you.

The ability to spot, focus on and manage Showstoppers is a critical corporate skill. Equally essential is the opposite: focusing on the Gamechangers, the opportunities than can create a quantum improvement in business condition. Problem or opportunity, winners in global competition push their organizations to discover the path most likely to result in a net increase in value.

2. MIX IT UP:

Agile uses teams, not departments. It lets project managers recruit the skills they'll need from other areas on a project-by-project basis. Some parts of this are better than others.

How do you manage production when your shop floor is 12,000 miles away? Management difficulty is the *bete noir* of offshoring: a recent Information Week survey found that 55% of CIOs were trying to avoid offshoring because of the difficulties in transoceanic management. But, in a competitive and capital-constrained society, avoidance may not be an option. You probably will be assimilated, whether voluntarily or otherwise.

The silver lining to all of this is that it is possible to

manage offshore projects effectively, as WalMart, Apple, Boeing and others have demonstrated for some time. But duplicating their success will require that you learn some new tricks and approach management from non-standard perspectives. There are several tools which have proved consistently useful in my twenty years of managing offshore fabrication projects:

Who Does the Design?

Many engineering groups work full time at keeping the non-engineers (or any other engineers) out of the process. The M.E.s, they're sure, know more about the processes, materials, and requirements than the rest of the idiots who try to put their two cents in …
It's not that simple.
There's one important spec that drives every project: WHAT WILL THE CUSTOMER PAY FOR? Much as engineers think they know the answer, they don't know nearly as much as the customer themselves. If the customer's involved early you'll find the problems early; if not, you'll find them when it's too late.
Of course, bringing in customers – or regulators, or channel buyers, or whoever – means extra management work. That's part of the job. Some extra hours up front are better than a blown budget and a career black eye.

Who's Running Your Production?

Due diligence has historically been difficult for companies moving fabrication offshore. Who is this guy I hired to run my facility? Does a fabricator who works great for WalMart work for me?
Performing due diligence has become easier in the past few years.Sourcing raters such as Panjiva provide

feedback for fabricators in fields ranging from apparel to toys. The Internet (and blogs) are also early warning systems for poor workmanship, slow deliveries, Imperial engineers, materials or specifications variances and other crimes against Nature.

Controlled Production

Mass production and scale economies sound like great ideas – until your buyers change their minds, you're stuck with inventory that you end up writing off or selling for 10% of production cost, followed by the Chapter Eleven or voluntary liquidation proceedings. The best way to avoid this when dealing with outside fabricators is to take a hint from the buyers at places such as Best Buy: create estimates/"production ladders" showing what you anticipate buying, but with no firm commitment made until you issue the actual purchase order. If the market's not as big as you thought, you don't issue any more purchase orders and you've got no further liability.

This is extremely functional from your standpoint, but will get resistance from your vendor – you usually need the market share and credibility of a Best Buy to make this stick, though it's always worth trying …

If your fab shop won't go for production ladders, there are alternative strategies to limit your exposure. The most common is to simply order small lots. This means that you won't get scale economies in your pricing – which is far better than being stuck with truckloads of goods that no one will buy after you've paid for them. Your vendor will press hard for larger orders, and remind you of the great deal you can get if you only ratchet up that quantity. (This is standard operating procedure in Asia, where

1920s mass production is still seen as state of the art ...
)   Listen at your peril.

If you've got the credibility, an alternative is negotiating a "put," where you'll give them that big order subject to your ability to (a.) pull out of any undelivered merchandise commitments immediately upon notice, or (b.) sell them back goods that haven't moved.   Unlikely as it seems, we've been in a couple of situations where the factory actually agreed to this.

3. <u>TALK IT UP</u>:

We keep coming back to communication, since it's so hard to have a real READY – FIRE – AIM system without it. This takes work. Dialogue, not monologue. Large portions of business communication are built around the "Imperial Proclamation" mode, which isn't particularly useful for any of the parties involved. "Parties involved" should include everyone who'll have a material effect on the issue. Depending on the specific concern, this could be:

Other managers
Line employees
Customers
Vendors
Regulators
Investors
(In some cases) Competitors

In operations, the first communication element you need to manage is definition: everyone needs to use the same words and concepts to mean the same things.

The Numbers: The parties need to understand how all elements will be measured. Management by adjectives isn't communication.

The Desires: What is each party trying to get out of the process? Within an organization, this is a straightforward process of outlining priorities and tradeoffs. (This requires the parties to think about priorities and tradeoffs, but that's not a bad thing for the business …)

Negotiations and discussions with outside parties (customers, vendors, regulators, etc.) get more complicated. Caution is called for – but too much caution can result in no one understanding what's being discussed. Outsider discussions, even between co-operating parties, always have a certain element of contract definition and a certain element of negotiating.

There's a school of thought that says the proper way to negotiate is to keep the other party completely in the dark about what you're hoping for. This is a grand and established tradition, running back to Sun Tzu and the T'ai Kung and all those Chinese scholar-warrior dudes.

At the risk of disagreeing with several millennia of tradition, my own experience has been that explaining what you want as early as possible saves everyone a lot of non-productive jockeying for position and fooling around. Contracting doesn't have to be an adversarial process, just a careful one.You probably don't want to let the other side know exactly HOW MUCH you want particular elements, or what your alternatives are if you don't get them, but until they know WHAT you want you're not dealing with the basic issues and have no idea if you're wasting your time …

The Deliverables: Who gets what when? People may not like the answers, but they need to know what's expected or all sides will be headed for much tedium, drama, and pseudo-legal grandstanding. None of this creates any value for the business (unless the business is headache remedies, in which case this is market-building ...)

The Feedback: If your vendors don't know how they're doing, they'll assume they're doing great. Honest, regular (but non-emotional) feedback is an essential part of making a sourcing relationship work.

The Penalties: What happens when the deliverables don't happen? This discussion should include what avenues of appeal exist short of calling the CEO, beating the crap out of each other in the parking lot, pistols at dawn, nasty comments on their Facebook wall or whatever.

When dealing with subcontractors or offshore fabricators, this can be crucial. Agreement provisions need to be worked out up front. This means (a.) they have to be in the contract language, and (b.) the vendors has to know they're in the language and that you won't pay for anything that's not according to the language.

Payment terms are important. The factory will try to get as much down as possible, so they're playing on the house money if there's a dispute later. The normal fallback position for them is half up front and half when goods go on the boat. We've pushed (often successfully) for an alternative:

a.   One-third up front. An alternative here can be agreeing that one-half is due and payable now, but paid as one-quarter sent now and one-quarter sent in sixty days. The idea here is to have them recognize that they haven't got enough cash in hand to make up for their production costs, and that you won't send them the money they're owed until they comply to the terms of the contract.

b.   One-third after shipping inspection. They've got their capital back by the time goods go on the boat, but you've got a reasonable assurance that you're getting what you ordered.

c.   The last third once your receiving people have accepted the goods. The factory makes a profit when they do what they've committed, but not before.

If there's a dispute, it's a good bet that the factory will try knocking off your goods and will attempt to get low cost clones into the U.S. under another brand. You should have a stipulation allowing you to legally stop such activity in the U.S. It doesn't mean they won't try, but it does mean you can seize the goods so none of the cloners make any money in America.

4. SET UP THE CIRCUIT BREAKERS:

In an uncertain world, you won't foresee everything. Your plan won't be perfect, and important issues will always be outside your control. You won't avoid problems, but you can have systems in place to limit the damage.

Modular Design

Avoiding mass production doesn't mean that everything is hand-crafted by Black Forest Elves. One method to reduce long term inventory exposure and improve sourcing of components in short supply is to design multiple products around basic components or ingredients. The components can be diverted to other products in the event that one turns out to be a sales dud.

This allows you more flexibility in securing ingredients or components that are in short supply. When a product category really takes off, this can be a serious problem. We were manufacturing an iPod peripheral device where there was an eight week backorder on a single part where no substitutions were possible. We managed to buy some parts from another fabricator whose product was held up for other reasons, but (a.) this raises fabrications costs, and (b.) means you're betting two months of cash flow on your ability to find someone whose procurement department was thinking further ahead than yours was and who's willing to bail you out of the problem.

An alternative strategy is the one we mentioned above: put in a large guaranteed order to be spread over a long period of time, which payments only made as lots are called for.

Tool Management

This is an area that can kill you in several different ways. The first happens when (as your vendor will always suggest), they own the tool that they fabricate as part of your order. Good luck getting your hands on the tool if you ever want to move the fabrication business to another vendor. However, after much weeping, gnashing of teeth, and hand-wringing, vendors will accept a separate order for tool manufacture where you end up with ownership of the tool, and can hold back payment to them until the tool is delivered into your hands or until the end of the production run – if you're willing to be obnoxious and persistent enough. Persistence is advised.

A larger concern, even if you hold the tool yourself, is the issue of single point failure. We were working recently on a pharmaceutical client where (a.) 60% of the entire production was dependent on a specific tool, (b.) they only had one of the tools, and (c.) replacing the tool was an eight-week process. The idea that their company could lose two months of cash flow if that tool cracked wasn't a priority with management. The analysis of risk – reward tradeoffs left something to be desired.

Asset deployment is a variation of this same theme. If your company owns subsidiaries, it may make sense to have the most valuable employees and equipment "owned" by the parent company, which then takes only most stable business and runs riskier (if more profitable) ventures in subsidiaries that contract back with the parent for needed resources. This limits the risk of a bad venture taking out the entire organization – but it requires a parent with enough foresight to organize ahead of time and to not guarantee loans for the subsidiary.

Multiple Production Lines

Since I'm standing by my aversion to mass production, the idea of actually having multiple production lines going remains a non-starter. However, that doesn't mean you shouldn't have plans for what you'd do if, for whatever wild and crazy reason, your current production facility wasn't usable. There are two issues that you can and should deal with in this regard:

a.	Pre-qualify alternative vendors. The moments of chaos, recriminations, threatened lawsuits and absurdity when you're terminating the current relationships are not the ideal time to be screening next year's model. It's better to work out your alternatives before you're desperate for them.

b.   Have a Conversion Plan: Improvisation is best left to the comedy workshops. You need a "break glass in case of emergency" plan developed before it's needed.

Inspection

How many times have we seen clients get containers of high-demand goods cleared through customs after weeks on the high seas only to find the goods inside were no damn good and would have to be sent back and replaced with stuff that actually met the #%@&*!!!!in' specifications while the end customers waited impatiently? Too damn many, I can tell you.

The time to find problems is not after the goods have already been shipped. In addition to all the irritations mentioned in the preceding paragraph, you'll also be faced with the two most deadly words in the language of international business:

AIR FREIGHT

as you squirm frantically to get product into the hands of your justifiably-annoyed customers. For those of you who haven't found out the hard way, air freight is about twenty times more expensive than ocean shipping. Unless you've got some pretty impressive gross margins, this is gonna hurt.

You need local (in the country of fabrication) inspectors. Most major Asian fabrication locales have companies who specialize in this and have cadres of degreed engineers, fluent in the local dialects, who'll be happy to inspect on site for far less than your own people are costing you. Actually, you need more than one source of these inspectors – it's only a matter of time before the fabricators try bribing your inspectors to let shoddy goods through, and known market competition for inspection (coupled with unpaid receivables that will stay unpaid until the goods have landed here and passed inspection) is one of the few ways to minimize the rampant corruption.

You need to negotiate inspection terms into your contracts with your vendors. These include:

a. Inspection on Demand: Your inspectors can show up at the factory without prior warning, pull sample lots of the line, and see how everyone's doing. (Note: This requires that the factory is giving you daily updates of progress on your order, which you should insist is a part of the contract.
You should also insist that financial penalties and/ or cancellation of the contract are authorized if they lie you about progress meeting the schedule.)

b. Inspection Before Shipment: Your inspector pulls samples and reviews final goods before loading them onto the boat is authorized. Schedule this time into your process: everyone will be wringing their hands about how short the turnarounds are and they've gotta get things moving NOW, but it's really far more efficient if you're sure the goods are right before they go on the boat.

c. Your Inspector is the Sole Arbiter of Problems: Many Asian fabricators are driven by their engineers, who have great power and often decide to unilaterally change specs "because they know better." The contract needs to state (i.) that's not allowed, and (ii.) if they do it, they won't be paid.

5. <u>KNOW WHERE YOU ARE</u>:

Agility is driven by knowledge. Immediate knowledge: the most important question for an Agile project is: "Where are you RIGHT NOW?"

Effective Agile projects often involve daily updates. The approach we often use for this is the "Ten Minutes Before Lunch" huddle, where everyone on the project gets together and puts together notes on the major project management concerns:

a. Is the project on track (and how do you know)?

b. What are the top five issues facing the project right now?

c. What is your solution for each of them?

d. What will you execute tomorrow, and what resources will you need that you don't have right now?

The notes are then sent to the executive in charge of the project, who can respond (or not) as seems appropriate. This will provide everyone with the information they need if the huddle is actually held to ten minutes.The more it overshoots the time limit, the less useful the information that comes out of it.

The structured information tools we discussed earlier offer important support in identifying issues and shifts early and locating the specific problems. A couple of cases in point:

- We've found that the Dynamic Costing analysis often highlights operational problems: the least profitable products or channels within a class usually have production or logistics problems which show up when their bills of materials, fabrication processes or logistical requirements are examined.

- Correlation of expense or profit shifts between G/L expense accounts often reveal production issues. We were working with a health products company which was having efficiency problems. We were able to identify a packaging problem specific to a certain class of containers on a single packaging line in Lugano, Switzerland before we ever hit a shop floor simply by careful analysis of the correlation between several general ledger expense categories. The value of financial data seen as ongoing processes rather than "snapshots of value" becomes very clear in these situations.

Structured Information approaches let us know what is happening with projects and ventures. Agile Operations techniques let us manage initiatives, even when they're distributed globally. The one aspect we haven't yet addressed: what projects should we be executing in the first place?

Great execution of poorly-selected projects won't build value. Value requires that we make the right efforts – and that means that we have to make the right decisions.

IX
DECISION TOOLS

Information won't produce corporate results by itself. The wrong actions, no matter how flawlessly they are executed, will end up producing the wrong results. Successful businesses, above all, need to make the correct decisions about deployment of assets, what markets and products are the highest priority; about what are acceptable risks and returns, and terms and conditions; about who should be fired or promoted, and what's the right price and what's the right purchase.

This takes more than a static projection and a PowerPoint slide show. Making the right decisions has always been something of a Black Art, part of the indefinable *je nais se quois* that characterizes the first-rate leader. It separates the top guys from the worker bees, the visionary executives from the mid-level bureaucrats.

This would be fine if we didn't see the first-rate leaders and top guys and visionary executives making crap decisions with such disturbing frequency. In a globally competitive, post-Meltdown world of Darwinian corporate conflict, we're in serious need of something besides the Divine Spark of grad school inspiration if your company's going to come through all of this with any kind of decent performance statistics.

WHAT DOES EFFECTIVE DECISION-MAKING LOOK LIKE?

One method for developing the best solution is to simply look at every possible solution to your problem and measure which one's the best. This is called the "Brute Force" approach, and generally works best when you've got several hundred million years to find your best move. Those of us operating on a shorter time horizon need to use a method to cut the time requirement.

Effective decisions result from a disciplined process. They involve systematic consideration of the factors that produce results. In corporations, "results" translate to "business value."

Effective decisions can be implemented. The resources required are small enough that generating them is economically and logistically workable – and the resources are accessible enough that decision support can be supplied on a regular and timely basis.

Effective decisions are focused. The process is directed at priorities, rather than creating a system where every action is paralyzed by detailed analysis.

Wherever possible, effective decisions are based on hard values. They generally involve numbers, since number-based tools allow us to explore our concepts of value and test our conclusions in ways that are difficult with less structured thinking. The history of business fads, of "synergy," "vertical integration," "matrix management," "scale economies" and all the other approaches that sounded good but were never proved out with specific performance metrics, stands as a warning to the alternative.

Effective decisions involve clear processes. These processes are tests or models to give us more clarity about the hunches, gut instinct, and street sense that are an incapable part of the decision-making process in real world business. They're driven by an ability to measure value with numerical scores, even for subjective measures. Numbers, not descriptions.

Michael Milken feels there are six factors driving value: (1.) the company and its management, (2.) industry dynamics, (3.) the state of capital markets, (4.) the economy, (5.) regulation, and (6.) social trends. While these are certainly strategic issues for a value-building CEO, they're difficult to include in daily executive decision-making.

My own experience suggests that, unless there are clear and quantifiable factors coupled to the value analysis, the ability for the company to weight alternative moves rapidly from the cloudy to the nonexistent. I've had the most luck focusing value analysis on four primary areas:

1. Problem Focus

2. Weighting

3. Pattern Matching

4. Alternative Selection

Considering each of these areas systematically helps executives move beyond reflex actions to more powerful decisions with less room for error. To see how this works, let's take a closer look at the process.

Frederick W. Croft

PROBLEM FOCUS

When we first think about critical business issues, the range of options seems to be enormous: thousands of potential moves even in fairly simple situations.This is what game theorists refer to as "combinatorial explosion," and it's a problem that pushes too many executives into the greatest mistake in management: doing nothing. There are so many solutions they can't pick just one.

The first step in developing a workable solution is usually to apply Karl Popper's Falsity Principle, which we discussed earlier. As you recall, Popper states that, while it's almost impossible to prove something is true it is definitely possible to prove most things are false. This gives us a place to start from: determining the things that will NOT be true about a workable solution helps us build a "filter" to knock out bad alternatives: if an alternative has one or more of the characteristics of a bad solution, it automatically bites the dust.

The methods for doing this reside in a branch of math and programming techniques called "heuristics." We're not going to get into any of the mind-numbing detail, but it's worth discussing a few of the concepts used in heuristics analysis that you can apply for yourself without whipping out a batch of Greek letters and C++ code:

- The issues addressed by any decision can be thought of as a list of factors.Scores can then be assigned for each of these factors (generally referred to as "weighting" them). If the factors are financial (revenue dollars, gross margin dollars, or whatever) the comparison's pretty simple: look at the highest dollared alternative as 100%, and consider other alternatives as the relevant percent of that. This is the probabilistic approach that Robert Rubin introduced at Goldman Sachs, and its use isn't limited to investment.

The same approach works for sales close rates, number of units sold, scrap rates, and other operating statistics. In any of these cases, you're moving from adjectives ("Alternative A is the best, but Alternate B sucks") to a specific measure of how great Alternative A really is and how much Alternative B really sucks.

The approach can still be used when dealing with subjective factors. You can create a number score for how much more stylish alternative a design is than its alternative, or how much more comfortable you feel in buying a particular brand.

- Collectively, this set of factors describing various aspects of an alternative can be thought of as "dimensions" of that alternative, with the set of dimensions describing the "location" of that object in a map of solution possibilities. You can think of this "map of solution possibilities" as something like a wrinkled bedsheet or 3D rendering of a mountain range: some areas will be high (i.e., the stuff with the highest scores which represent better alternatives) while others will be in valleys (i.e., bad solutions that you'll want to avoid).

- These dimensions are useful in figuring out potential Showstoppers, building factors that will show you how you're wrong when you're actually operating the plan you've chosen. (As you probably expect by now, you WILL be wrong – but good indicators will tell you where …)

Heuristics consists of various methods using math to sort through this "solution landscape" to find the best option.Serious heuristics use a lot of math and a lot of computation: sorting through the thousands of options requires processing power. This makes it a poor choice for many business situations, since the folks on the line or out there negotiating sales terms – the people who are driving much of your business value – aren't ever going to sit down with the calculus and a hot VBA-wired spreadsheet. But there are alternatives.

WEIGHTING

Let's go back to that measurement issue, to weighting of the various factors. This has become a fundamental part of management over the past decade, and there are several commonly-used approaches.

Perhaps the simplest is the "probabilistic analysis" used by Robert Rubin at Goldman Sachs that we've already discussed. But, at the risk of sounding like some business version of von Moltke, the determining factors for (a.) what's working tactically, differ from those affecting (b.) what works strategically. Most firms use different tools than Rubin's. In decision support systems, the most common tool for determining what works in tactics is something called "Key Performance Indicators," or "KPIs." The tool for what works in strategy is called "Balanced Scorecard."

KPIS

Key Performance Indicators are the metrics most businesses use to measure their operating successes. There are several elements which characterize a good KPI:

- KPIs can include both financial and non-financial indicators.

- The KPIs have a generally agreed and pre-defined association with a particular business process.

- KPIs enable you to set clear and quantified performance goals for the business process in question.

- KPIs let you use a quantitative/qualitative measurement of results for the particular business process. (If it's qualitative, you need to figure out how you'll weight it and use it.)

- The result of the KPI process must be specific action(s) which improve business value. If performance measured by KPIs doesn't lead you to taking an action (whether it's popping a champagne cork or slitting your wrists) you've got the wrong KPIs.

KPIs get good and mis-used in many business environments. Many KPI efforts don't follow the guidelines noted above; company executives pick a few phrases that sound good and convert those into the metrics they'll use to run the business. A LOT of metrics. We've seen situations where the monthly metrics reports ran twenty pages with over one hundred KPIs. They could save themselves the trouble and have NO KPIs – nobody in the company is bothering to read any of them NOW when you've got dozens of them.

I'm recommending that you dust off the Telephone Number Rule and hold the total number of KPIs to seven or less. This gives at least some chance that people will be able to remember enough about your KPIs to use them to build useful results.

Several common problems get cited when people write about KPIs:

1. It's hard to build agreement on which KPIs to use. Rembrandt didn't go for audience participation, and you shouldn't either when you're setting KPIs. Personally, I've always found that ground zero for at least some KPIs is their linking to key financial factors: when you're operating a for-profit business which requires capital, the money factors have to make it into the final cut. This doesn't address intangible/intellectual property factors, which are important in a lot of businesses. If you're going to have KPIs for these, you need to think about useful KPIs – activity (i.e., filing patents or releasing new products or mentions in the media) doesn't automatically build company value, so you need to decide what DOES.

2. The KPIs are hard to track. This is often the case, which is a sure sign that people weren't thinking very hard when they chose their indicators in the first place. If you can't track it and relate to something specific, you can't use it for anything.

3. Once KPIs are set, they're hard to change. In a rapidly changing world, this is a problem – fossilized key management indicators can lead to business paralysis.

BALANCED SCORECARD

You can't tactically manage your way to greatness. The long term doesn't take care of itself and DOES require that you manage it effectively.

The idea with Balanced Scorecard is that you can set up a sort of "value statement" that will help you track progress in addressing strategic issues. It was popularized by Robert Kaplan and David Norton (who did some of the early development work on activity-based costing, after it was originally developed by TI in the early Seventies). The theory is that the scorecard gives businesses a control mechanism for projects building intangible value, addressing potential for inflection points, and other issues that aren't reflected in traditional financial statements. The approach has been used successfully by corporations ranging from Mobil Oil and CIGNA Insurance to National Bank OFS and AT&T Canada.

The original idea with Balanced Scorecard was that you incorporate various quantitative measures combined with abstract measure of "true importance to the enterprise" to develop a broad-based "strategic management system" that will be used to focus and co-ordinate the corporation's efforts in these areas. The initial approach created tables to rate corporate performance in four primary areas:

1. FINANCIAL

2. CUSTOMER

3. INTERNAL BUSINESS PROCESSES

4. LEARNING AND GROWTH

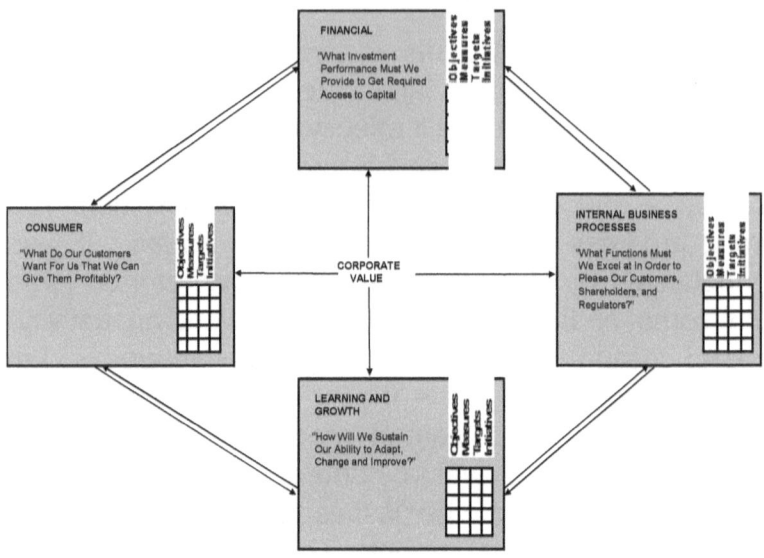

This immediately drew fire from innumerable backseat drivers asking "why those four?," "Hey, I've got another one!," "You should've used mine!" and other expressions of puzzlement, jealousy, irritation, bemusement, disgust, and Sartrean nausea as are common throughout most decision-making processes. Responding to all the fooraw, Kaplan and Norton came up with the "New!, Improved!" system, something called "Strategy Maps," which states that, just as you can't manage what you can't measure, you also can't measure what you can't define (see my earlier comments above).Strategy mapping then sets out a process to:

- Clarify strategies and communicate them throughout the organization

- Identify the key process drivers for success

- Align investments in technology, people, and capital expenses for the greatest impact, and

- Expose gaps in the company's strategy that must be addressed

HOW WELL DOES THIS WORK?

Some of the larger companies using Balanced Scorecard have racked up respectable performance numbers (though naysayers wonder how much of this is attributable to the process). There's also some naysayer concern that this method isn't based on any proven economic or financial theory, and Balanced Scorecard is ultimately a subjective process which looks at various issues without providing a bottom line score or recommendation.

There's a Rule of Thumb (remember our rule of thumb about Rules of Thumb) which says that half the balanced scorecard initiatives will fail in three to five years, and business researchers such as Gary Hamel (in a *Fortune* article from 1997) have raised numerous complaints about balanced scorecard content and application:

1. "No visibility" into drivers.
2. Subjective weighting of drivers
3. Unresolved driver conflicts
4. Scorecard doesn't prioritize improvement opportunities
5. Doesn't assess operating constraints
6. Scorecard encourages short term view
7. Scorecard effort can't sustain under adverse conditions
8. Scorecard gives weak co-operation incentives

It's hard to satisfy some people.

The concern we've seen with both KPIs and Balanced Scorecard/Strategy Map approaches is that they're often not actionable. You get some sort of indication that you're making some sort of progress in some direction. Correctly designed KPIs do give you some idea of what's causing the problems when you don't achieve your targets; Balanced Scorecards are less successful in this.

They also require a recruiting and sales effort inside the company. One man's perfect KPIs are another's extraneous noise. Toolmaking isn't a popularity contest – but getting tools to be accepted IS.

WHAT SHOULD I BE WEIGHTING?

Most human processes, from baseball to attractiveness as entertainment icons, have their established operating metrics. The key question about most operating metrics – and particularly the question about business metrics and dashboard content – remains "is this stuff valid?"

Baseball isn't a typical business, but is a case in point. The well-known *Moneyball* sagas of Billy Beane and Bill James, who built high-performance teams with low-performance funding, show the utility of shifting from "industry standard metrics" (batting average, RBIs) to statistics that correlated with team success (i.e., getting on base). Since they didn't have the balance sheet of the Yankees or other teams who could spend whatever it took to get the players they wanted, Beane and his Oakland A's had to get the most useful players they could afford (a very different approach requiring very different measurements). By correlating useful stats that other teams didn't track, they got a lot for their recruiting dollar by going after under-valued player characteristics.

The validity of this approach is argued in baseball and just about everywhere else on the planet. One of the arguments is the "correlation doesn't equal causation" argument that we've all heard. That's a true statement – but it overlooks the fact that correlation may indicate a deeper issue worth examination. The correlation isn't cause, but it IS potentially valuable input.

The other major objection is that historic performance statistics are so dependent on numberless tiny elements of the real-world situation that it's hard to extrapolate from them. True as far as it goes – but analysis from poor data is generally more useful than analysis from no data, and the performance of the A's with Billy Beane (or the performance of the Boston Red Sox when they adopted a similar approach) compared to the A's pre-Billy Beane suggests there's a deeper causation underlying those particular correlations.

Baseball has a set scoring system, so there's relatively little debate about what constitutes "bottom line" effectiveness in baseball. Business also has a bottom line, which is ultimately value (the long-term share price of the company being managed) rather than the actual bottom line, which doesn't address intangibles and strategic issues that drive the share price.

The intent of any decision system, therefore, is to produce an assessment of business value created by an option which can be compared to one or more business values created by other options. Since this is business, the bottom line for all of these value assessments is risk-adjusted rate of return. This involves quantifying:

- The parts that produce rate of return

- The rate of return itself

- The range of probabilities that the return will actually happen, and

- The downside if you select the option and it doesn't work

<u>Working Parts</u>

The "parts that produce return" are those that (a.) produce cash flow streams (which have a long term value as would a similarly-risky bond), or (b.) that can be sold, just as we recall from introductory finance classes. This excludes large portions of most business operations (as we saw when considering "non-value added" and "required" issues with Lean). Different scenarios often have different working parts.

<u>The Rate of Return</u>

One of the first elements of a business-oriented value weighting process is to consider the true assets which are available under a given scenario/option:

1. The operating value of an asset, which is (a.) the free cash flow produced by the asset in question, which includes the cash receipts coming in less the operations cost required to produce receipts going out, multiplied by (b.) the multiple, which works the same as a price-earnings multiple.
    The multiple creates a "price" for that free cash flow stream which is equivalent to the price for other similar investments and, in effect, looks at the asset as though it were a bond with a risk rating. (Hopefully, this process works better for the asset valuation than it has for bonds over the

past few years …)

The operating value of the asset will vary depending on the scenario. Business options often include selling off some assets (or closing down asset operations) to finance the purchase of others. This changes cash flows produced, the multiple used on various cash flows (cash from a one-time sale obviously doesn't get a multiple), and

2. The value of any assets which could be sold under the scenario. This obviously doesn't include any assets used to produce the free cash flow stream. It may also need adjustment depending how quickly you need the sale to take place under the scenario: "liquidation price" for an asset is usually a fire sale, hardball situation which yields considerably less than "orderly liquidation price," plus

3. The cost of implementing the scenario. This can include purchase of new assets, paydown of debts, development efforts to produce new products, new promotional campaigns – any money going out in an effort to change things for the better.

The Range of Probabilities

You've probably heard that nothing's constant except change. This affects your consideration of alternatives. The Great Worldwide Meltdown gave us a look under the hood at the subject of Operating Risk, which was pretty much swept under the rug for decades as everyone concentrated on the seductive pseudo-certainties of the "snapshots of financial value" in financial statements.

Risk is a huge subject which we'll only touch on here. However, there are a couple of risk-related issues which are so fundamental to analyzing value that we need to take a closer look. Basic operating risk issues (not to be confused with insurance, benefits, or most of the stuff people think about as "risk") includes:

Understanding of Commitments: This is an issue we examined while discussing Agile Operations. The "social contract" isn't some Eighteenth century idea from Jean-Jacques Rousseau; it's a basic factor driving everything that gets done in business. One side agrees to deliver something, and the other side agrees to "purchase" it with "consideration." (Since the parties may simply be people in different departments of the same company, "purchase" may simply be accepting the product or service in question as being acceptable to be passed along to the next department, and the "consideration" may be nothing more than an agreement that the first person has done their job). This process affects all of your interactions in business:

With customers
With vendors
With bankers
With shareholders
With other employees
With professional peers
With regulators
With media

If you define what you will deliver (the performance, accuracy limits, materials used, finishes, etc.) and what you WON'T deliver (the operating limits, warranty exceptions, limits on merchantability and all the rest), life will work much better than if you do what too often happens and make some vague, poorly-articulated, undefined and undocumented agreement that will be misunderstood by both sides and result in anger, slander, threats, and general excessive drama. This should be avoided.

Single Point Failure Elements: Remember our snappy little parable about my client with the single tool? The company that was risking $10 to $12 million in cash flow to save a $20,000 tooling fee? The company whose CEO responded to the question of whether the firm would survive if they took the cash flow hit with a rousing "Hell, no!"

It's a good idea to understand what can kill you before it does. "Single point failure" is even more often an issue with key people, who can walk out the door with proprietary and poorly-documented trade secrets in the time it takes for them to punch up Monster.com and locate another employment option. Since employment follows that well-known principle of economics called Gresham's Law (Gresham said "bad money drives good money out of circulation" and I'm saying "bad employees drive good employees out the door"), the best people have the easiest time moving to another job and leaving you with a roster full of the terminally lame and annoying.

Product Lifecycle: I mentioned my recent work with a cellphone peripherals company. Phones are a fashion-driven product, whose interfaces shift continuously as they try for more features and more consumer lock-in. So my consumer electronics client looks more like a fashion house, with the average lifecycle for a product running between ninety and 120 days. In the hyper-competitive environment of the post-Meltdown marketplace, every industry looks more like the fashion industry. If you don't plan for this when figuring out how you'll get to market, how you'll control manufacturing excesses, and how fast you need to get payback from the product, you'll be seeing more red ink than a Coca-Cola label printer.

Process: Bad production erodes value. Re-work, excess scrap, and unsold inventory all reduce free cash flow. Unstable manufacturing processes drive up labor costs and wear on machinery. The basis of Six Sigma (reducing variation) is a real issue in creating or losing business value.

The Unexpected: These include Acts of God (fire, earthquake, extraterrestrial invasion), Acts of Lawyers (endless lawsuits that can chew up years, distract everyone involved and cost zillions), Acts of the Mentally Handicapped (which can run anywhere from terrorists to PETA, presuming those are two separate categories), and Acts of Politicians (which range from brainless regulations through value-destroying tax policy, and, now that I think of it, could probably also be lumped under Acts of Mentally Handicapped). As the Astronomer said at the end of *The Thing*, "Be Vigilant! Watch the skies!"

VOLATILITY AND YIELD

Yield from a business option is normally determined through a financial projection of the option's forecasted results. As you'd expect, the projection doesn't come with a guarantee that it will be anything close to accurate. Making it as accurate as possible involves managing several issues.

Smoothing

Projections are built from historical financial data. This historical data often has its little problems. The process of whacking this raw data into shape is called "smoothing."

The theory here is that periodic entries are "spikes," "shock losses," "anomalies" or other phrases suggesting that the elements being described are oddball, once in a lifetime, nonrecurring quirks of a quantum reality. In theory, these need to be adjusted so they don't distort your projection. But there's often a question as to how shocking the shock losses really are, and you need to make sure your smoothing process isn't rewriting history. Mandelbrot has identified several instances where "smoothing" results in "making up data" and creates easily-analyzed patterns that have little relationship to the raw input.

There are several statistical tools which are used to create mathematical smoothing. The classic method is something called curve fitting, which takes the actual numerical experience from previous periods and uses "least squares" or other math tools to determine a curve which closely approximates the past.

The curve is then extended forward to create a future estimate. This assumes that the future will look like the past, which doesn't always work out …

Another common method is regression, in which the prior period's numbers are increased or decreased by adding or subtracting a specific number (linear regression), or multiplying them by a specific percentage (exponential regression). This can be used to develop an overall growth rate. Since most businesses experience seasonality (their operations sell more or less at different times depending on holidays, number of days in a month and other factors), a "multiple regression" approach may work better if you've got enough data points, fitting the data of each month to the regression model that's most comparable, and then tacking the set of individual monthly regressions into a "mosaic" of trailing regressions to create a composite curve. The mosaic is then expanded using the overall growth rate to create the subsequent year's projection.

Regressions are not without their problems. When limited data points are available as the basis, you can often find the situation where any of several different curve patterns fit your data: is it really linear, or exponential, or something else entirely? (The 'coefficient of determination" or R-squared, test distorts with limited data points or complex growth curves.) The other issue is that regressions keep rolling forward with the same growth rate as long as you keep pushing them. This is unlike the real world, which often moves forward for a while and then plateaus (the phenomenon that some paleontologists have described as "punctuated equilibrium"). Extended sufficiently, this produces the dread "hockey stick" curve that showed up frequently in the business plans for bad Internet start-ups but seldom in the real world.

There are also more complex math tools that can be used. One that's been used in several recent analyses of financial markets is replicating string series. Again, this assumes that market movement consists of a lot of random noise overlaying significant events. Think of a stone being thrown into a lake: the general slight ripples on the surface are overlaid with a defined pattern of period ring-waves.

Like those rings, market events often consist of a series of similar "ripples" in the consumption or pricing patterns. There are various math "filters" which can be used to sort out the random variation. If what's left shows a defined pattern, it may be the early stages of a replicating string series (a series of sequential data elements is often referred to as a "string"), and can be a signal that you can use to adjust your marketing efforts accordingly.

Fractals, the math behind all those splashy CGI graphics in special effects movies, can also be used to smooth data and extend it forward. Again, math filters remove the random noise and (when the remainder closely matches a fractal set) the fractal can be used as the normalizing tool.

(Note: A number of years ago I worked with fractals when I was involved with the start of Altamira Group, a software startup which used fractals to enlarge digital images. We were able to extract data in the enlargement that wasn't in the underlying photo negatives using this process – a similar process to that used by NSA in imaging from spy satellites. The same techniques work in developing data curve patterns …)

Sounds pretty damn scientific, doesn't it?

The real world is never as clean as this makes it sound. Several analysts have pointed out the weaknesses in many analytic tools (correlation and regression being the most common targets), and most of their concerns are valid.

How does this affect our analysis?

For one thing, all of these methods work better if there are lots of data points. But financial expense data aren't booked daily; you've usually only got workable data monthly (since accruals are booked at the end of the month, and since most large sales are closed at the end of the month), so you'll have to take a limited number of data points and make them work.

For another thing, there are limits to how big a

company's market penetration can grow. There's also a change in profitability as companies reach market saturation. You've probably heard people note sadly that their projections prove "the road to Hell is paved with a hockey stick curve" such as you get from many regression-generated projections, and the problem can take place with any of the systems we're looking at here. Checking the ratios for competitors that are similarly-sized to the market share you're projecting is often a valuable reality check for the projection process.

The issue isn't Platonic perfection. The issue is finding a plausible starting point for decision-making. Math tools produce a starting point that's potentially more valid – and certainly more salable to your organization – than Ouija boards, laudanum-induced trances, flipping coins or reading the corporate horoscope. Any of these (horoscopes and coin flipping included) would actually accomplish something valid (i.e., getting your analytic thinking out of a rut and looking toward alternatives you've ignored as unthinkable, ridiculous or absurd), but decision systems need to build consensus as well as stimulate analysis.

Missing Data: Often the only way that you can get enough individual data points to build a solid analysis is to combine several sets of data. Frequently, the data sets will have a gap between the end of one and the start of another. Regression, replicating string series, and fractals can all be used to fill in the curve so that it doesn't have gaps.

Product Lifecycle: Your company won't work just as it does now when it's one year later. Hot products will be less hot. New products will mature, and you'll have to figure out just how quickly this will happen. The trend analysis tools that we discussed above will help with this. The trickier part remains guessing how new products will perform. Modeling new product performance off combinations of similar products you've released and other peoples' products that you're trying to emulate can be useful, but doesn't come with any ironclad guarantees.

Scenarios and Sensitivity Testing: The classic approach to sensitivity analysis (determining how stable your financial projection results will be when the real world throws you some changes) is pretty simple: run the projection assuming ten percent more (and ten percent less) revenues and see what happens.

This is a solid approach as far as it goes. But the key element here is understanding what drives change, and what you should be watching in the real world to find out where you're wrong. Models are useful in showing you HOW things change: how the relationships between parts move when the revenue input is altered. But you need to understand WHY, to identify the Showstopper factors in your strategy assumptions to plan ahead for shifts in debt covenants, up-front requirements for business growth, and other issues that will be stranger than you're seeing them.

MAKING TRADE-OFF DECISIONS

Let's assume for the moment that you've passed on coin flipping or meditation as decision drivers. What do you use?

Making business decisions is ultimately driven by the need to make tradeoffs. Option A is more likely to pay off – or is likely to pay off better – than Option B. The core issue is "what is the realizable value of each alternative, as described by a simple risk-adjusted value calculation":

(Probability of Success x Value of Success) –

(Probability of Failure x Cost of Failure) = Realizable Value

This leads us to the question where most of these systems blow a fuse: what's "value"? As we discussed earlier, value can be a lot of things. One of the things it seldom will be is a pure GAAP (or IFRS) value. Value is partially driven by potential, positive or negative. It's also driven by intangibles, and we're not making value-based decisions until we've accounted for all of these issues.

For the past half century, a growing body of work has focused on methods for weighting alternatives and choosing the best option. These have collected under the label "game theory," and, while many of the working parts in classic game theory aren't very practical for most corporate operations, I'm taking the position that game theory approach is worth a closer look.

WHAT THE *@&%#!!! ARE WE DOING HERE?

Whoa! Hold your equine quadrupeds! About now you're thinking that I'm being awfully damn inconsistent with all that stuff about unpredictability and quantum reality we looked at earlier. Game theory? Fractal patterns? Replicating string series and regressions? How do know that any of this stuff isn't just random oscillation, and how do we know that any "scientific" theory of decisions has any validity?

Okay, here comes the answer: WE DON'T.

Management must manage, which means that management must make a lot of pressure decisions in situations where they have very little idea of what's really going on. Inaction is the surest route to executive failure, so you have to do something, even when it has good odds of being something *wrong*.

The key to being an effective manager is recognizing this is the case – and making the decision anyway. Great managers (like great generals) often achieve greatness (or at least survival) by their interventions, quick fixes and goal line saves, not by their initially fantastic conceptual brilliance. The key to effective management is also identifying the specific measurements, indicators, flashing red lights and blazing sirens or whatever that will tell you that you're wrong and you need to make changes NOW. Ready – fire – aim.

So make that lousy decision. Live with it, and be ready to change it when you get better input. With that in mind, back to our regularly-scheduled programming.

GAME THEORY 101

Most of us recall game theory from various *War Games* reruns and Prisoner's Dilemma scenarios. We don't recall it from on the job experience, since corporate uses have been limited. The limitations tell us a lot about managing strategy.

Classic game theory, the von Neumann/Morgenstern stuff, started with some premises:

1. Two players
2. Zero sum (someone totally wins, while the other side totally loses)
3. A single "game" determines everything

There aren't many situations that work like this in the corporate world (or any other world, for that matter). The playing field is so artificial that it's not useful.

There's been quite a bit of rubbish circulated on this subject – we've all got assorted images of Dr. Strangelove, Matthew Broderick as a dial-up hacker entering the Strategic Air Command, and various mechanical-brain-takes-over-the-world movies from the Fifties rattling around in our memories – which is to be expected considering Game Theory's Cold War/Whiz Kids origins. Let's get beyond that and think about what failures here tell us about decision systems.

The basic concept of Game Theory is simple: it's a tool that walks the user through alternatives in a systematic, numerically weighted manner, and – WITHIN THE CONTEXT THE USER PROVIDES – helps them see which response provides the logically-strongest outcome.

You've probably picked up on all the landmines and smoke and mirrors embedded in that last sentence. Like all analytic tools, Game Theory is only as good as the user. However, the approach has some attractions:

1.   It's numerically based, which gets us away from all the really, really subjective, adjective- and emotion-based foundations of much social decision-making.

2.   It allows us to make analyses quickly. Once you get used to the approach, you can fill in the assumptions and get a result in very little time. This is important in corporate situations, where decisions are often made under time pressures.

3.	It gives us a consistent analysis process. We can improve our ability as users through a ready-fire-aim process.

This ties into the weighting approaches we discussed earlier, suggesting that there's something here that's more practical than initial appearances would suggest – if we can find it.

HOW DOES GAME THEORY WORK, ANYWAY?

Game Theory is driven by a couple of inputs:

a.	<u>The Decision Tree</u>: This is what it sounds like: all of the possibilities, in the order which the decisions must take place, laid out graphically and connected to each other in a pattern looking something like a tree to those who have severe vision problems.

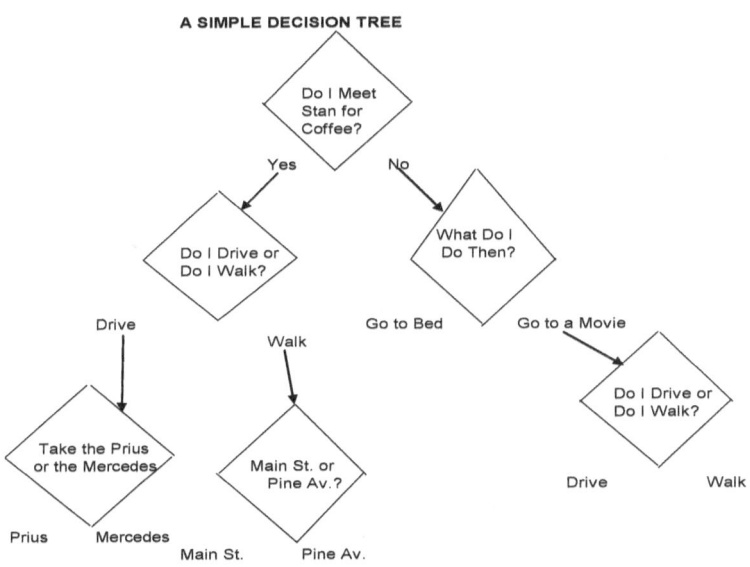

But it gets hard to see the conceptual forest for the decision trees in many real world examples. As you can see, even the simplest of decisions tend to have kittens: most real-world decision trees involve dozens or hundreds of options, which means the problem has to be expressed carefully or you get spaghetti instead of a visual tool.

b.   Truth Tables: These are scoring tools, sets of "points" accumulated by each of the "players" in each different possible scenario. The truth table scores allow the user to determine who "wins" in each instance, which in turn determines the effectiveness of each strategy.

Defining decision trees and awarding truth table points are both subjective exercises. One of the reasons that game theory has limited usage in non-military organizations is this subjectivity, which can make the models unstable. Let's look at an example.

THE KIDNAP GAME

The Kidnap Game was a concept developed at the Rand Corporation think-tank by Daniel Ellsberg, whose grasp of game theory didn't keep him out of mucho hot water with the Federal government when he leaked the Pentagon Papers to the *New York Times* a few years later. The Kidnap Game works like this:

1. Albert kidnapped Bob and held him for ransom. The politically-ambitious D.A. is foaming at the mouth, and wants to make an example out of the dirty kidnapper to stop this stuff once and for all. He'll

go for the "Little Lindbergh" death penalty for kidnapping if they catch him.

2. The ransom's been paid, and Bob's sworn to keep silent about Albert's identity if Al will just liberate Bob, so everybody can forget the whole thing and, as Rodney King desired, all just get along.

3. Albert has to decide (a.) whether he trusts Bob enough to let him go, or (b.) if it's safer to kill Bob and thereby keep his (Albert's) identity secret.

In the classic Ellsberg model, Albert's best strategy is always to kill Bob:

a. It's always as good a strategy for Bob to tell after the fact as it is for him to remain silent.

b. Albert has to, therefore, assume that there's a risk of that death penalty if he releases Bob and Bob tells. Albert doesn't want to kill Bob, but he also doesn't want to face the death penalty by being caught.

c. If he kills Bob when Bob would've been silent anyway, Albert didn't lose anything: he would've been facing the death penalty anyway if he were caught.

d. If he kills Bob when Bob was planning to talk, Albert has kept his identity secret and is therefore better off than if he'd let Bob go free.

The diagram (with non-viable scenarios crossed out) is shows as follows:

CLASSIC KIDNAP GAME

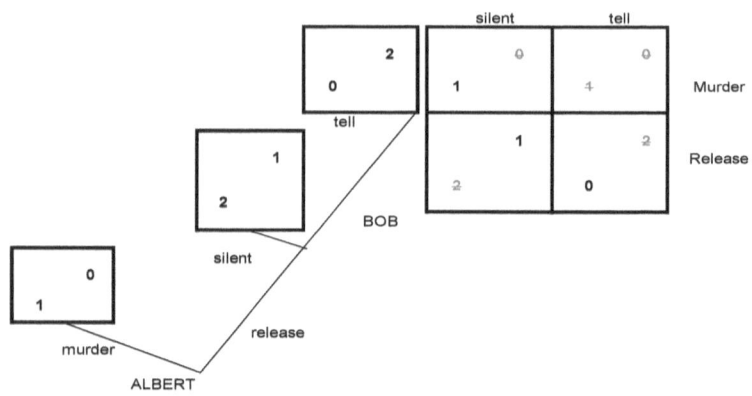

That's the classic Ellsberg scenario. But this classic scenario has some problems.

The first is the assumption that there's a constant penalty for being caught, regardless of the crime you're caught FOR. In this model, Albert is always facing the death penalty – his only question is whether he escapes completely or is totally screwed. A lot of game theory models work this way (it cuts down the branches on the decision tree), but the real world is another matter entirely. Kidnappers routinely receive lesser penalties than kidnap-murderers, and their trade-off analysis has to take into consideration the benefit of a lesser punishment in the event they exercise mercy.

The other piece of this is the degree of trust between captors and victim. To see how this plays out, let's consider a similar real-world situation: the Patty Hearst kidnapping by the deranged, lunatic, media-obsessed and slogan-spewing terrorists of the Symbionese Liberation Army (the "SLA"). In this situation, Hearst – as Designated Representative of the Capitalistic Oppressors – was abducted by a batch of middle-class "revolutionaries" and not-too-smart criminal types who held her captive to force her Evil Capitalist Oppressor family to contribute food to the downtrodden, hoping this would be the opening gun in a Revolution of The Masses™ against said Evil Capitalist Oppressors.

Patty's family went along with all this and contributed food to folks who at least claimed they were downtrodden, receiving generally positive media coverage as a result. (The SLA apparently failed all their "Understanding Media" courses in junior college, since it didn't occur to them that having every media outlet in the Solar System broadcasting news releases saying (i.) the Hearst family were doing the right thing, and (ii.) the SLA were a batch of terrorist psychos, wasn't the greatest revolutionary propaganda coup in the history of insurrections.)

The SLA were actually so dim that they weren't motivated by the penalty differential we just discussed: they saw themselves as part of a Vast Historical Movement that would ultimately win them eternal fame as Liberators of the Proletariat, so little things like death penalties for murder were only a minor distraction. This was not good news for Patty Hearst, but it wasn't the end of the analytic situation, either.

In game theory terms, what actually happened is a variation known as Cozy Kidnap. (When your initial model doesn't play out in the real world, always declare that the actual event is a "variant" so you can preserve the credibility of your analytic process ...)   In this approach:

1.   Hearst convinced the SLA wackos that she was a fellow revolutionary at heart, needing only their superior socio-politico guidance to lead her to a true Revolutionary Conscience. For Patty, this scenario beat the Cheez Whiz™ out of being shot as an Enemy of the People, so she went for it.

2.　　From the SLA perspective (such as it was), having a live Patty Hearst as a fellow revolutionary and living illustration to the downtrodden masses that their revolution was actually viable from a conventional citizen's perspective was more valuable than any limited dismay that The Man would've felt due to her execution.

3.　　Having Patty accompany them of various criminal hijinx also made her a fellow criminal, which made it more likely that she'd stay committed to the "revolution."

4.　　They decided that Patty alive was worth more than Patty, dead, and she kept breathing until the SLA was sufficiently riddled with reactionary, law enforcement bullets for her to escape.

　　Suddenly, the game theory analysis breakdown changed to the following:

HEARST KIDNAPPING

All of this shows the sensitivity of models to just a few changes in assumptions and value weightings. Models are always caricatures; they aren't the world itself.

INPUT AND GAME THEORY

Is there anything useful in all of this?

The classic Ellsberg and von Neumann models share a characteristic: they are all single snapshots of an ultimate outcome. (Reminds you of a balance sheet, doesn't it?) Like the other stiff, single point analyses we've considered, these models require that you get everything right the first time and know everything there is to be known.

The real world isn't this simple:

- Instead of two "players" there are many.
- There are multiple runs rather than a single game (which changes strategy for participants, since a "betrayed" player in game one can "pay back" their betrayer in additional rounds).

When these factors are built into the gaming/ analytical process, we get very different games. John Forbes Nash (the *Beautiful Mind* guy) laid out the basic model with the well-known "Nash Equilibrium." A set of strategies is a Nash equilibrium when no player can do better by unilaterally changing his or her strategy. To test a situation, you can imagine what would happen if each player were told the strategies of the other players. If any player would want to do something different after being informed about the others' strategies, then that set of strategies is not a Nash equilibrium. If, however, the player does not want to switch (or doesn't care if he switches or not) then the set of strategies is a Nash equilibrium.

Practically, this means that over time multiple players will, by making the best decision for their own position, arrive at a closely-related set of positions which oscillate back and forth in a relatively narrow range. When something seriously changes the situation, there comes a round of rapid, large oscillations which drop back to an equilibrium once everyone understands the new situation.

The complexity of these situations reminds us of another analyst of real-world games: Karl von Clausewitz. Like Nash, Clausewitz noted that most decisions are made with limited information: the "best" data that's generally out there. Clausewitz notes that basic information is obscured in what he called "the fog of war": the confusion, distortion and misdirection which emerge from the chaos of real world disputes. He observed that "war requires only simple tasks, but even the simplest task becomes immensely complex" on the front lines in the midst of what he called "the friction." His student von Moltke noted a natural result of this, the fact that "the first casualty in any military action is the plan of battle."

Clausewitz' deductions still remain valid after two centuries:

- Success in conflicts is largely driven by a rapid INITIAL concentration of overwhelming force against a specific objective. Strategies focus on the starting point, with the tactical line commanders adapting dynamically to develop a final victory.
- Success is a function of the speed of execution. Faster is better because it's less risky. There's less time for NEW unknown factors to be added to the unknown factors that are already there that you've missed.

These concepts suggest several rules of the road for our development of portfolio management models:

1. Weigh, don't predict

2. Measure original position and weigh alternatives, don't try to predict outcome

HOW DO WE MAKE THIS WORK IN REAL LIFE?

In one major test, players using game theory didn't do any better solving real world problems than other student-opponents. But game theory produces several results that are useful for executives:

a. It gives us a numerical way to compare different tactics/strategies

b. It gives us components that can be checked against subsequent results to understand where our model failed. (Note: I'm assuming that the model WILL fail, because models ALWAYS fail. Their use is in telling the executive where the problem lies and where his initial assumptions were mistaken ...)

Standard game theory models solve for a consistent strategy (or set of strategies, in "tit-for-tat" models where an opponent's initial behavior determines the type of response used by your side) that will win the entire game. This requires a simple game if you want to keep the number of decision tree branches below the number of atoms in the State of Nevada. Getting the strategy model right for every step in the game in you initial analysis is unlikely.

But solving the entire game isn't necessary in business. For corporate decision-making, we need to solve for *the strongest single move at a particular point in time.* Getting enough information to create a complete best strategy at the onset of the game is unlikely – this is a situation where ready-fire-aim is more likely to succeed.

Working within the frame of corporate management gives us a huge advantage when compared with management of the twisted psyches of revolutionary wackos such as we saw in the previous example. All of the players are going for the same goal: quantifiable economic advantage. We don't have the equivalents of the moral/political/psycho/sociological considerations that drove the decisions in the Hearst example. We can follow the money.

The focus on economic advantage also allows us to simplify the number of values we're analyzing. Economic success is driven by the traditional factors we've seen for years in net present value and risk-adjusted earnings calculation. There are four elements which are consistently applicable to these calculations:

1. Current State:
    For modeling results of a financially-driven organization (i.e., all human organ-
izations that are doing anything consequential), the first step is the find the "whole value," the "enterprise value." This will consist of the tangible assets that we see on a balance sheet: cash, accounts receivable, net equipment value – all the stuff that can be quickly monetized.
It will also include intangible items. The most important of these will be the value of the free cash flow produced by business operations (in excess of the value of the equipment used to produce it). This value is usually valued by looking at it as though it were a bond (i.e., an

ongoing stream of payments) and assuming what price a sensible buyer would pay to purchase that series of payments. (In my illustrations here I've translated this into an "earnings multiple" similar to the "price-earnings ratio" that many readers will have already seen in discussions of stock prices. It's just as valid to look at price from the other direction, as a reciprocal of the desired interest rate – choose your arithmetic.)

Intangibles also include the sale price of patents, brands or copyrights, which is theoretically related to a stream of payments but which may have a different value for another player (i.e., a large company who could do more with your patent than you can) than it does for you. Intangibles can also be sales channels (for many consumer products, getting shelf space in key retail outlets is a critical issue) or key contracts.

What they're NOT is contingent items: tax loss carryforwards, proceeds from lawsuits, the potential impact of unexercised options, etc. These may be included on financial statements for GAAP purposes, but cloud up our analysis of what the company's CURRENTLY worth. If the future lawsuit proceeds or carryforwards have a verifiable market, this might be a different issue. Otherwise, they'd be treated as "Changes," which we'll address in the next section.

The result looks something like the following example:

CURRENT STATE		
NET TANGIBLE ASSETS		
* Cash		100,000
* Accounts Receivable		650,000
* Salable Assets (orderly liquidation value)		250,000
INTANGIBLE ASSETS		
Free Cash Flow x multiple (less assets used to produce it)		100,000
	x	8
		800,000
		(650,000)
[Net]		150,000
[Patents, copyrights] - sale value over free cash flow multiple		-
[Sales Channels] - sale value over free cash flow mult.		-
[Brand] - sale value over free cash flow multiple		-
TOTAL CURRENT STATE ASSETS		*1,150,000*
LESS LIABILITIES		
Accounts Payable		(200,000)
Credit Line		(250,000)
TOTAL CURRENT STATE LIABILITIES		*(450,000)*
CURRENT STATE VALUE		**700,000**

2. Change:

This is the proposed change in the situation from where we are now. It could be litigating or not litigating, hiring an employee, closing a facility, buying a useful patent – anything. We're taking the economic value of the change (i.e., cash flow produced – or saved – by the change times economic value), LESS the cost of making the change. The result looks something like this example (showing the impact of that patent purchase for illustrative purposes):

PLUS THE CHANGE
Develop Patent - New free
   cash flow from patent over
   next five years $50,000/yr.
                        x   5 yrs.
                           250,000

Less cost of patent
   development   (100,000)
CHANGE VALUE   **150,000**

3. <u>Risk</u>:

This includes all of the areas where your plan can (and probably will) go wrong; where your forecast misses a critical element, your staff can't execute, the market doesn't really exist, or you're smitten down by an Angry God. For this analysis, we need to consider (a.) how big the loss will be, and (b.) how likely the loss will be. For our patent example, it would look something like the following:

LESS RISK

Loss if patent doesn't work   (100,000)

Times probability   x   .2
RISK VALUE   **(20,000)**

4. <u>Timing</u>:

  The longer something takes to pay off, the less it's worth. Net present value approaches generally figure a cost of money and deflate the eventual worth of the project. This is another negative number.

  When you combine all of these elements, you can develop a risk-adjusted value. This can be compared to the risk-adjusted value of other alternatives, as is shown in the following example:

OPTION A - STAY THE COURSE		OPTION B - DEVELOP NEW TECHNOLOGY	
CURRENT STATE		**CURRENT STATE**	
NET TANGIBLE ASSETS		NET TANGIBLE ASSETS	
* Cash	100,000	* Cash	100,000
* Accounts Receivable	650,000	* Accounts Receivable	650,000
* Salable Assets (orderly liquidation value)	250,000	* Salable Assets (orderly liquidation value)	250,000
INTANGIBLE ASSETS		INTANGIBLE ASSETS	
Free Cash Flow x multiple (less assets used to produce it)	100,000	Free Cash Flow x multiple (less assets used to produce it)	100,000
	x 8		x 8
	800,000		800,000
	(650,000)		(650,000)
[Net]	150,000	[Net]	150,000
[Patents, copyrights] - sale value over free cash flow multiple	-	[Patents, copyrights] - sale value over free cash flow multiple	-
[Sales Channels] - sale value over free cash flow mult.	-	[Sales Channels] - sale value over free cash flow mult.	-
[Brand] - sale value over free cash flow multiple	-	[Brand] - sale value over free cash flow multiple	-
TOTAL CURRENT STATE ASSETS	1,150,000	TOTAL CURRENT STATE ASSETS	1,150,000
LESS LIABILITIES		LESS LIABILITIES	
Accounts Payable	(200,000)	Accounts Payable	(200,000)
Credit Line	(250,000)	Credit Line	(250,000)
TOTAL CURRENT STATE LIABILITIES	(450,000)	TOTAL CURRENT STATE LIABILITIES	(450,000)
CURRENT STATE VALUE	**700,000**	CURRENT STATE VALUE	**700,000**
PLUS THE CHANGE		**PLUS THE CHANGE**	
Don't spend money on the new patent opportunity	-	Develop Patent - New free cash flow from patent over next five years	$50,000/yr.
			x 5 yrs.
			250,000
		Less cost of patent development	(100,000)
CHANGE VALUE	-	CHANGE VALUE	**150,000**
LESS RISK		**LESS RISK**	
Damage if competitor develops the patent opportunity and takes business		Loss if patent doesn't work	(100,000)
[lost cash flow]	(30,000)		
[over 5 yrs.]	x 5		
	(150,000)		
Times probability	x 30%	Times probability	x 2
RISK VALUE	**(45,000)**	RISK VALUE	**(20,000)**
LESS TIME LOAD		**LESS TIME LOAD**	
5% per year applied to change revenue	-	5% per year applied to revenue w/patent taking 3 yrs. to come to market	
		[net cash flow of $150,000 less 5% per year times 3 years]	(23,644)
		applied to risk w/loss w/in one year [loss of $20,000 less 5%]	1,000
TIME LOAD	-	TIME LOAD	**(22,644)**
WEIGHTED SCORE	655,000	**WEIGHTED SCORE**	807,356

The accountants in the audience will observe that I've simplified the timing adjustment from the ideal: in theory, the timing adjustment would be phased over each cell – day, month, hour, or whatever – in the period.

This is one of the many instances where simpler is better: we're trying to create a system that will work in an actual business environment. Realistically, this means a system that a non-financial staff member can apply for themselves in 30 seconds or so, which allows the system to become part of ongoing corporate decision-making practice.

Of course, the example we've shown above is still pretty complicated. Suppose you simplify it.REALLY simplify it. For each option, the user assigns scores to each of the four elements: current state, net upside shift in assets, the risk – and cost – of failure, and the cost of timing. Normally, the scores are assigned subjectively with a 1 to 10 scoring base, with 10 being the most intense and 1 being the least intense.The scores are picked subjectively by the user, going by what "feels right" rather than a specific calculation. (As we noted earlier, management is driven off "relative values" rather than any mystical "true value.")

So what does that look like?

OPTION A - STAY THE COURSE		OPTION B - DEVELOP NEW TECHNOLOGY	
CURRENT STATE	10 points	CURRENT STATE	10 points
PLUS THE CHANGE	0 points	PLUS THE CHANGE	3 points
LESS RISK	-1 point	LESS RISK	-2 points
LESS TIME LOAD	-1 point	LESS TIME LOAD	-2 points
WEIGHTED SCORE	8 points	WEIGHTED SCORE	9 points

I'll admit this is fairly subjective. I'll also admit that ANY analytic process is going to be subjective: the purpose of such an analysis is to arrive at a plausible starting point FAST (so you start with slightly less likelihood of dealing with issues that are just stupid, as opposed to unforeseen) rather than foresee an "ultimate truth."

Having a useful tool that's really simple encourages the line employee to analyze the problem when they first encounter it, which means issues are being addressed as early as possible. The goal is to make a considered decision that builds the user's best judgment of specific areas; this isn't a precise calculation because (a.) a fast decision is usually more useful than a slower one that comes too late to be used in the decision process, and (b.) most decisions involve areas that are hard to quantify with total accuracy – all decisions will be approximate rather than perfect.

For employees who aren't used to working with financial statements and numbers (let alone actuarial or net present value considerations) this is a quick way of touching all the bases and coming up with a reasonable choice. Filling in the plan matrix takes less than a minute, and requires no financial training. If two employees (or an employee and their supervisor) run the same analysis, they can compare differences in the weights to cross-check their assumptions and to use it to communicate concerns. The tool helps both parties understand how they're making decisions.

TIMING AND RISK

In more detailed analyses, one of the issues that should be considered in more detail is risk. The reason for this is simple: risk doesn't remain constant over time. The longer the period of time being "forecast" (i.e., the length of time it will take a project, business initiative or whatever to be completed), the more unknowns can creep in between the forecast's "best guess" and the eventual reality. More unknowns normally translate into greater risk that something will come up that's unforeseen in the analysis.

A common example that we've all seen is the yield curve: a 30-day Treasury bill yields a lower rate of interest than a five- or ten-year bill. The differential is the market's estimate of this increased risk over time. But the market's risk estimate may not be applicable to business situations. Markets in US securities don't include any default risk, though they increasingly price to the estimated redemption date (which can be earlier than the redemption date, and lowers the value of total interest payments that will be made) rather than the scheduled date of redemption. In business, many products and operating ventures will have a more limited working life – this can be as little as eighteen months to three years. (Look at television shows, music or fashion – how many three-year old products/programs/musical acts have any relevance?)

Venture capital rates of return blend the risk of default with the risk of unknowns over time that we're discussing here. Bond market rates are probably more useful (is your new venture the equivalent of unrated debt? Of factoring?), and recent data is more readily available.

PAST PERFORMANCE IS
NO GUARANTEE OF FUTURE RESULTS

Plans don't come with guarantees, and there's no insurance that will protect an executive in every possible circumstance. Identifying Showstoppers and operating metrics is as important a part of the decision-making process as selecting any particular scenario. The best plan is often the one that positions you to survive when it fails.

X
EXIT, PURSUED BY A BEAR[1]

How do you come out of a restructuring project alive?

Theory doesn't count until it's working inside your organization. And making it work isn't easy when everyone hates change, everyone fears the future, and (since you're the change agent) everyone hates your guts. Strong measures are required.

When facing issues of such magnitude, I tend to rely on the time-tested methodologies. REALLY time-tested, in this case. The ones used in the Renaissance.

I refer, of course, to Niccolo Machiavelli, a hands-on change management executive, and a man so adept at implementing these issues that he wrote a best-selling handbook for change management during a period when the status quo was officially labeled a reflection of the Will of God. His recommendations won't make you popular, but they will (a.) make you successful, and (b.) keep you alive.

---

1   This is my favorite stage direction (from Shakespeare's "A Winter's Tale"). The reference isn't to bears or bulls, but to the fact that (a.) we're all pursued by various hostile and inhuman factors at any given time, and (b.) it's time to exit.

Machiavelli noted the difficulty of life as a change agent up front:

"There is nothing more difficult to manage, or more doubtful of success, or more dangerous to handle than to take the lead in introducing a new order of things."
The Prince,
Ch. 6

This is so because:

> *"A new prince must always inflict harm on those men over whom he rules … Thus you will always find enemies in those who you have injured by occupying that principality."*
Ch. 3

He further notes that, while your enemies are white-hot to do you wrong, your supporters are "lukewarm," because they operate:

> *" …partly from fear of their adversaries who have tradition on their side, and partly from the incredulity of men who do not truly believe in new things until they have had a solid experience of them."*
Ch. 6

What a downer! But, since we all accept that management must manage, we as executives must overlook the unpleasant implications of all this and move forward to develop methods for creating corporate transformation in a world that runs with these operational constraints.

Long and sad experience in companies facing the need for corporate transformations has led me to several observations about the working environment therein, which is dominated by several strong emotional themes:

<u>Fear</u>: Everybody in the place is afraid that one of three things will take place regarding them personally:

- There'll be more lousy decisions made by management (after they've already seen management make some poor ones), and they'll be left holding the bag,

- The lousy decisions and work they've personally made or done in the past will no longer be swept under the rug; they'll be found out, and retribution is at hand.

- They will be blamed for someone else's lousy decisions and work done in the past when some sly and manipulative co-worker decides to either dodge a bullet for their own incompetence, or to remove a potential competitor in the department.

This makes them surly.

<u>Nostalgia</u>: The past that everyone detested when they were actually living in it suddenly looks like the Lost Golden Age as they realize:

- It may have been lousy, but it was EASY. Everyone knows how it works, and there aren't any ugly surprises.

- The people doing well in the old situation have nowhere to go but down in the new one.

This makes them resentful. Once they see that the transformation project won't go away simply because they ignore it, we see the next round of reactions:

Hysteria: The minute a change project is started, it faces a number of reactions which are as predictable as the sunrise and the Law of Gravity:

- *"We've gotta get orders out the door!"* The old favorite: we'd LOVE to go along with you, but there's this overwhelming crisis right now, so we can't possibly get to any changes until the terrible crisis is over. Of course, all the problems and inefficiencies stay in place so the crisis is never over – which is what they really wanted, anyway.

- *"We know what we're doing!"* It is a sad fact of the Universe that there's One Infallible Sacred Truth: when somebody forcefully and self-righteously tells you "We've been here for [fill in a double digit number] years, and we know what we're doing!," that's absolute evidence that they're complete idiots who haven't got a clue about their job or anything else.

- *"The workers aren't ready for change yet!"* This is a sign that the SUPERVISORS aren't ready for change, which often means that the actual workers are chomping at the bit for revisions in processes they know damn well are stupid, dangerous, expensive, ineffective, or all of the above.

You can plan on similar reactions to your organizational change projects. Human nature being what it is, these reactions are pretty common. If you're brought in from the outside to fix one of these things, these reactions underscore the need to have your scope of action defined UP FRONT with the folks who brought you in. You'll never be in a stronger position than when they're trying to recruit you – and, when you're a change agent, you'll never be in a position where you don't need all of the latitude you can negotiate for yourself.

The negative emotions condense rapidly into several immediate resistance moves, usually within the project's first week:

1. Inertia: People start giving new projects the Richard Nixon Memorial Dose of Benign Neglect. The projects don't move.

2. Undermining: Various general comments are circulated about the lack of competence, ethics, etc. of the new order. (This is pretty common, and change agents are advised to acquire the thickest of bulletproof Kevlar skins if they intend to make a career of this stuff.)

3. Escape Attempts: Complaints are made to the Board and/or the CEO, coupled with attempts to suggest other operating structures if they won't come to their senses and fire the change agent. Again, this is par for the course in organizational change projects.

ARMED RESISTANCE (AND ITS REMOVAL)

Machiavelli advises that *"all armed prophets have been victorious, and the unarmed ones have come to ruin."* (Ch. 6) If you don't act rapidly, you'll lose the option of acting at all and others will be driving the agenda for you.

Machiavelli suggests three possible options in these situations:

a. Scrap the Company

b. Take Firm Control, or

c. Exact Tribute, i.e., let them do what they want so long as you get a sufficient return on capital

The first option isn't too popular with shareholders, since it travels hand in hand with red ink and humiliation throughout the industry.

The third option sounds interesting, except for the fact that, if they can't actually deliver, the managers run down the value of the company's asset. (Since most corporate assets are priced on discounted future earnings, the value of the asset goes down if they can't deliver the earnings …)

This leaves us with "take firm control."

Machiavelli advises that firm control means just that: you move in and settle things as thoroughly as possible:

> *"Men must either be caressed or destroyed, because they will revenge themselves for small injuries, but cannot do so for serious ones."*
> Ch. 3

"In taking a state, its conqueror must consider all those cruelties which he has to do and do them all at one stroke, so as to not renew them every day ...
Ch. 8

"It is much safer to be feared than to be loved."
Ch. 17

This suggests that the successful transformation leader will have to be firm; have to be implacable, and often needs a well-chosen show trial and execution [i.e., termination of the person leading resistance to change] at the beginning of their administration if the leader's going to avoid chaos. Sad but true – and unpalatable for many potential leaders. All of this suggests caution is required when selecting the transformation leader.

The key is to be firm but fair. Ivan the Terrible will fail, but giving quantitative goals – and enforcing them – is perfectly acceptable. You move to assign goals as early as possible, often within the first thirty days of the restructuring's start. You then enforce their delivery.

The classic example of this was Jack Welch and GE: he'd get project leaders, up front, to commit to goals **and agree on measurements**. And he'd follow up. Don't deliver the goals, and you've already agreed that you'll suffer – so, once people saw that Welch meant it and people really would suffer – they got motivated and made changes, whether from self-preservation or from more noble motives.

Welch wasn't popular, but he was effective. And he kept on getting results once he made the first project work, because he remembered that – just like Deming and Juran advised us – improvement is continuous, so you keep re-setting the goals once the first one has been met.

IMPLEMENTING TRANSFORMATION

Why does it have to be so difficult?

People don't like to be measured. They don't like being accountable. They're still in love with Management by Adjectives.It's unpleasant to face any of this, but, as Machiavelli reminds us, it's a lot less pleasant to face layoffs, company sales, career death, and all of the unpleasantness that travels with the alternatives.

The motivational counters to resistance – fear of collapse, coupled with the call to the glamour and adventure of a Big Turnaround Success – must be coupled with a careful selection of the team leader for the initiative. Let's take a closer look at the consensus-building process.

FOLLOW THE LEADER

You need a clear and present danger if you're going to be aggressive in moving for change. There's usually one available if you look around, so do enough research to find it before you start. And you need someone to lead the Charge of the Light Brigade against it.

There's often a difference between the actual leader and the person whose name is at the top of the org chart, particularly when there are bullets flying. If you draw the short straw and have to save the world by yourself, you'll need to proceed systematically.But that may not be your best move.

Once you've identified the problem, you need to find the right leader and get them to agree with you. The careful agent of change will look at this as a multi-step process:

STEP ONE:
RALLY THE TOP

Any transformation process will get nowhere without active support from the top of the company. Since the top of the company was in charge while the problems developed, this requires some careful positioning.

An obvious psychological model for this situation is the twelve step process for substance abuse, where there's also a tendency of participants to understate problems and postpone the reckoning. The twelve step process assumes several factors always apply:

- Admitting that one cannot control one's addiction or compulsion;

- Examining past errors with the help of a sponsor (experienced member);

- Making amends for these errors;

- Learning to live a new life with a new code of behavior.

Until these factors are accepted in company management, it's difficult to create any progress. In substance abuse, this is often catalyzed by intervention, where outsiders – concerned family members and friends – emphasize the necessity of change. In business, intervention generally comes from three outside sources:

1. Banks,

2. Shareholders, or

3. Key clients

Those are folks you don't want to involve. By the time you're getting this input from any of these sources, your business has serious problems – and involving either banks or key clients creates the risk of massive new problems in funding or sales. How do you move the needle short of this?

If the company's having problems, the CEO is probably interested enough in hearing ways to improve things. The CEO won't want to ADMIT there's a problem, but he'll usually be nervous enough to recognize that one exists. Getting him to act usually takes three things:

1.   Evidence, which usually consists of downward-trending statistics regularly updated and supplied over a period of time,

2.   A suggested way out, and

3.   Enough time to convince him that the problem won't solve itself and he has to act.

Since few CEOs get or hold the job without (a.) a healthy dose of paranoia, and (b.) the ability to read simple illustrations of depressing numbers, sooner or later this will have an effect.

The key problem – if you're not the CEO already – is getting to the CEO without being killed by the nervous (usually under-performing) senior managers surrounding him like a sincere-suited and conservatively-groomed Praetorian Guard. There are several ways to get the idea through the middle management barrier, most of which work better if handled as anonymously as possible:

a. Convince your boss that this is an opportunity for him: This is an area where company politics can work for you, since your boss may find it useful to lead the charge and weaken some of his opponents. The key issue here is to make sure your boss is close enough to the top to speak with the CEO directly: trying to follow this route through nine layers of assistants to the assistants won't work and will probably get you killed.

b. Get the concept directly to the CEO: If your boss is too nervous, you don't have to follow in his gutless footsteps. Write the thing up and get it to the CEO directly. You can be modest and not sign it if you're really, really worried about retaliation.

c. Contacting a Board member as a concerned shareholder is a last resort. This requires real caution. You should try your boss and your CEO before taking this route. If you contact a Board member who's representing a large share bloc (a.) they'll probably be even more nervous about performance than you are, since they're already reading the bad news in quarterly filings, (b.) they'll be more impatient with a "stay the course" strategy, and (c.) they won't be at all afraid of anybody in management. They'll be motivated.

But CEOs will be nervous about any subordinates contacting any Board members for any reason. Sending ideas unsigned is by far the safest option if this is your only recourse. Once the ideas are viable at the Board level, you can jump on the bandwagon since you already understand much more about the solutions than all the deadbeats who were dragging their feet while things fell apart.

STEP TWO:
SELECTING A TEAM LEADER

This is a tricky decision. A change leader who's successful in transforming the company can gain significant stature in the process IF THEY SURVIVE. Survival's always the problem, since all of the threatened mid-level executives will hate your guts for getting them into this transformation thing, and will do their best to make it fail so they can get back to the idiocy that's gotten them where they are now.

If you're really strong, really good, really lucky and really self-confident, you can blow them off and go for the brass ring. If you're more inclined toward self-preservation, you may consider having someone else take the helm of the project once you've gotten it on the slate:

a. This provides someone else to take bullets, and

b. It may be a way to recruit another ally. (You'll certainly need all the allies you can get).

There are several candidates for this role in most organizations:

1. <u>An old Senior Statesman who wants one last victory before retiring</u>: If you can find someone like this, they can be VERY useful. An older division manager or senior VP probably has his own relationships with the CEO and Board members. He's not scared of other players since he's already decided

to leave, and may want to leave a legacy through the transformation project. Older executives may not be the innovative type you'd first think of to lead this effort, but they'll be seriously motivated to make it work (if only to protect their retirement plan-financed Golden Years).

An older manager has credibility with the most traditional factions in the company since he's been there so long. And he'll be scarier than Hell to the opposition since they know he's got nothing to lose. All good. He'll take most of the glory, even though you end up doing a lot of the work. But you'll be the Anointed Successor – to say nothing of being the only one left to pick up the pieces once he's been put out to pasture.

2. <u>A young hotshot who wants the glory</u>: There are times when it's useful to let someone else – someone courageous and hot to make a name for themselves, to say nothing of someone who may not be reading the deeper implications of the situation – lead the Charge of the Light Brigade. It's better to be Tennyson and write the poem than to be one of the legendary dead guys who inspired it. Hard-charging young heroes are often amenable to suggestion that the company needs them, and only them, to save it in this Hour of Gravest Peril. If they can actually do it, you've got a New Power in the company who sees you as one of his team.
If they can't do it, you had someone take the shot in the head for your side, leaving you alive to fight another day.

3. <u>A consultant who's paid to take the bullet</u>: Many of my clients take this option. (Lucky me ...) It requires very overt sponsorship at the CEO/Board of Directors level, but can be very effective while keeping the top guy's hands clean from all the hideous (if necessary) unpleasantness that usually travels with transformations. It also gives you a credible outside moderator for the intervention.

This approach has some advantages for the change agent: the job gets done, someone else gets killed, that someone isn't around to be a long-term political threat, and the consultant/leader's outsider status makes it harder for the resistance to figure out how to stop them. The main issue is giving the consultant enough support so they won't be stonewalled (see "Richard Nixon Memorial Dose of Benign Neglect" above.)

STEP THREE:
KEEPING IT CASUAL

Most successful change agents manage a difficult balancing act: emphasizing the size of the problem while appearing casual about how the company responds to it. This is counter-intuitive, but real; the inevitable opposition gets more intense the more it sees that the project is important to you. If it's important, you'll fight to create the change, and all the people wanting the status quo will fight just as hard to stop you.

If you keep making suggestions while choosing your battles (and supplying suitably threatening facts to the decision-makers), your opponents may not understand how serious you are until you've succeeded. You may also simply wear them down if they figure that (a.) you'll keep up, but (b.) the project won't make any important changes anyway. If the process is described in reporting or process documentation terms – and if it's driven by non-financial people who position it as an analysis process rather than an overthrow of the company's decision process – this is more likely to happen.

A common method for doing this with information is the ever-popular "we're only testing this out, so we want your feedback" pitch, which implies that this is only a test and that there's any chance in Hell that things will go back to the old ways. (And, occasionally, someone may actually have some good feedback that you incorporate into the system ...)

To see how this works in practice, lets' consider implementation of a Dynamic Costing project. Any change affecting financial data will generate opposition from Controllers, who (by nature) are always willing to cut expenses but extremely resistant to changing the ways expenses are measured and analyzed. This is definitely true of Controllers faced with costing analyses and statements by object. They will fall back on GAAP standards, claiming that other approaches "aren't right." This makes the preservation of the untouched GAAP data – and the reconciliation of the Dynamic Costing analyses to the general ledger detail – vital or the transformation will face entrenched opposition.

Dynamic Costing should be positioned with Controllers as a set of reports, not an alternate reality. More persuasively, it should be positioned as an alternative to micro-slicing the Chart of Accounts to build similar analyses (which is an option that's frequently suggested). Once Controllers are reminded of how much extra effort their department will go through in transaction coding if a Chart-centered approach is used, they'll usually prefer Dynamic Costing's "separate set of reports" approach.

If Dynamic Costing is then assigned to the cost accountants this is even better, since it avoids creating additional work for the staff building the financial statements (which most Controllers see as the "real" job of finance). Most cost accountants are more focused on assembling Cost of Goods numbers for the statements than on activity-driven analysis, but they're usually familiar with activity-based concepts and sympathetic to the objective. Many of them are also strong spreadsheet users, which is even better.

For structured information projects in other areas, the first hurdle is getting access to technical manpower:

- In Operations, Quality Assurance often has people who are used to working with numbers and specifics. The key issue is getting them to move from specific tests and procedures to more large scale analysis.

- Sales departments often have someone called a Sales Analyst or Sales support staffer. If this person has enough math capacity they can be used as extra hands, and can be credible program evangelists. If not, you'll need to get people assigned from Finance, which is often a turf war problem. Your biggest asset is the desire of Sales management to be efficient. Sales is a results-driven discipline, and Sales executives are often the easiest people to recruit for the approach IF they're shown that it's worth diverting resources from "feet on the street."

- Marketing, Engineering and Product Design are, strangely enough, the toughest departments to get bought into structured information. This is surprising, since all of them are driven by quantitative elements – but there's a creative/talent aspect with the way these people see themselves that builds a huge bias toward a hand-crafted, inspiration-driven work style.

Operational changes need to be led from the line. This means hands-on efforts, working closely with supervisors and opinion leaders (the "old hands" who are respected by the other line workers).   You need their buy-in to make operational shifts that work.If the process gets their legitimate input, and if they understand the genuine improvements that continuous improvement methods and Agile techniques have brought to other top companies and can bring to them, the "old hands" can shift to becoming your biggest supporters.

It's key that this is an "apprenticeship" approach, where the team leaders work hands-on with the line employees to demonstrate the value of the new methods. There are lots of operational consultants who handle the instruction as classroom-style presentations away from what they were shown after a few days in the classroom, and haven't seen how to couple ideas with execution. That doesn't build skills or commitment to the process. The project leaders need to drive the process from the locations where it will be executed, and make sure that the line employees can do the processes (and not just answer questions about them).

In any corporate area, the requirements for a successful transformation are similar:

• Create a large enough sense of urgency – immediate assignment of goals, agreement on measurements, and on consequences for non-performance.

- Find the right champion

- Move fast

- Make sure everyone under-estimates the importance of the project until you've got it running.

THE LAST WORD

Those of us who are lucky enough to serve as chief executive officers have an opportunity, even with all of the regulatory and funding limits we must work through, to achieve remarkable things. This is particularly true in the present time.

We have a rare management opportunity in the wake of the failure of old methods and failed business practices. Many old barriers and foolish preconceptions have collapsed. The way is open to build more effective businesses, to create real value in the organizations we run, using better tools to create better results for all of the stakeholders. Quality = Efficiency = Profitability. There aren't many areas in the world where people have a shot at doing something that's deeply meaningful – but this is one of them.

Maximizing this opportunity requires an executive who's self-confident enough to live without "standard operating procedures" and "industry standards" and all the other rubbish that caused problems in the first place. It requires comfort with ongoing uncertainty. The Ready – Fire – Aim process is an executive requirement in evolving and globally competitive businesses, which means that you'll never really know whether you're going to succeed until you do.

But the opportunity to create meaningful improvement has never been more real. Lean and Agile techniques have highlighted the amount of inefficiency that exists in the average corporation – there's a real potential of more than doubling output from corporate resources. This lets us create value, and build more interesting, challenging and high-achieving work environments for our fellow employees while we do so.

Let's make the most of our opportunities.